THE GUY'S GUIDE TO POCKET KNIVES

Badass Games, Throwing Tips, Fighting Moves,
Outdoor Skills and Other Manly Stuff

Mike Yarbrough

Published by:
Ulysses Press
P.O. Box 3440
Berkeley, CA 94703
www.ulyssespress.com

978-1-61243-717-0 (hardback)
978-1-64604-443-6 (trade paperback)
Library of Congress Control Number: 2017938180

Printed in the United States
10 9 8 7 6 5 4 3 2 1

Acquisitions editor: Bridget Thoreson
Managing editor: Claire Chun
Editor: Shayna Keyles
Proofreader: Renee Rutledge
Front cover design: Justin Shirley
Cover artwork: © coprid/shutterstock.com
Interior design: what!design @ whatweb.com, Jake Flaherty
Interior art: see page 183

NOTE TO READERS: This book is independently authored and published and no sponsorship or endorsement of this book by, and no affiliation with, any trademarked brands or other products mentioned within is claimed or suggested. All trademarks that appear in this book belong to their respective owners and are used here for informational purposes only. The author and publisher encourage readers to patronize the quality brands and products mentioned in this book. The operation of knives in this book involve a degree of risk and require a degree of skill. It is the reader's responsibility to ensure that he or she understands all such risks and possesses all necessary skills. Any decision to use the information in this book must be made by the reader on his or her own good judgment. This book is sold without warranties or guarantees of any kind, and the author and publisher disclaim any responsibility or liability for personal injury, property damage, or any other loss or damage, however caused, relating to the information in this book.

To Granddaddy.

Thanks for that first knife, and the honing of my character.

CONTENTS

CHAPTER 2
Know-How. 52

INTRODUCTION

For as long as I am able to remember anything, I will never forget getting my first pocket knife. I was seven years old, and a small boy for my age. I had just stepped outside with my granddaddy—I was always on his heels—onto our bit of country land, observed by the oaks and barn, when he reached into his pocket and handed me a small, antler-brown pocket knife. It was a significant event to me then and has remained so to this day. Something happens to a boy when he receives such a thing. He is being told without words, "You are trusted to be a bit dangerous." And when this acknowledgment of budding manhood comes from a figure he respects, he grows a little.

Many are the boys who have had such an experience, and, in generations past, they would have been ushered into schoolyard games and hours spent whittling. They would have been taught the importance of keeping their knife clean and sharp, and the sharpness of their knife would have been seen as a statement of character, carrying as much weight as a well-maintained lawn or home does in our modern age. So common was the knife that men wouldn't ask, "Does anyone have a knife I can use?" Rather, they would say, "Jim, hand me that pocket knife of yours," or, "Say, you got your knife on you?" with the certain expectation that you did.

The pocket knife is more than just an implement for opening boxes, or a rapid deflation device for angry ex-girlfriends to use on their former lover's tires; it is a statement. In its honed edge we learn about a person's skill and regard for their tools; in its appearance, a bit about their style; and in its functional design, we see forethought and readiness for the work to be done. Much like an old cobbler may know the steps of his customers by the soles of their shoes, a man's pocket knife tells a story. The knife that is passed down from father or grandfather to grandson has a story as well, and though it can never fully be told, it can be felt. That familial connection to one's ancestors and the thought of belonging to a history, as well as a unique point in time, does a heart and mind good.

In the same vein, there is currently a generation desirous of tradition and connection when most seem to be fading away. For a generation that has been raised in a toss-away world of cheap plastics, the thought of an item being purchased, used in earnest for a lifetime, and passed on to another generation is rare, noteworthy, and grounding. The time-honored ritual of passing along articles of remembrance, like the pocket knife, can start again.

Since boyhood, it has been a rare season in my life that I have not carried a knife with me. As a youth growing up in the country with plenty of time on my hands, I whittled anything I could imagine, though most of what I could imagine were weapons: spears from old broom handles (or from brooms that looked old enough for me to use and my grandmother not to miss), bows and arrows, slingshots, and the like. In this way, I became comfortable with a knife in my hands. And in the hours spent piling shavings on the porch, a good thing happened, which I believe kids are missing out on today: My hands stayed busy, and my mind was free to think. The value of this has not been lost on me; it's a true contrast from the activities of my peers, who stayed inside watching TV and playing video games. What seemed to me as simply a way to pass the time was critical in my development, and equipped me with a certain lifelong handiness and quietude.

As is common with most boys, I went through a collecting phase, in which I collected a number of knives. The ones that stand out to me are Rambo's knife from the movie *First Blood* and a fantastical beauty designed by Gil Hibben called the Double Shadow. It should be noted that no one thought I was a burgeoning psychopath simply because I liked knives, nor was it unusual for us to bring our knives to school and show them off during recess; a knife was simply a commonplace part of life. Sadly, most of the knives I collected in those years were lost or broken, but the pocket knife has remained a staple.

Along with a wealth of things to do with knives, this book will inform the reader of the history and proper maintenance of the pocket knife. For the purposes of this book, the term pocket knife includes a locking single blade with a pocket clip. While your grandpa's pocket knife was likely a small, multi-bladed beaut that jingled with the change in his pockets, most of today's carriers prefer a clip knife. (There is likely some philosophical point to be made over the cell phone having taken the place of honor over the pocket knife, but I'll leave that one for your own ponderings. I suppose it could also be noted that while the pocket knife was displaced, it was not completely worked out of a man's attire, but instead refitted to meet the demands of the age. I believe this was a prudent move, as field dressing a deer would be quite a difficult task with an iPhone.)

The intent of this book is not only to inform, but to inspire, so that the swell of knowledge and pride in this noble tackle will be too much for one lifetime, and must be carried on by another.

—Mike Yarbrough

CHAPTER 1

EVOLUTION OF THE KNIFE

"A knifeless man is a lifeless man."

—NORDIC PROVERB

As we peer through the ages of manly history and literature, we see the pocket knife taking a backseat to its august brothers, the sword and the dagger. We know the tales of Excalibur and Carnwennan, King Arthur's sword and dagger, as well as Tolkien's Andúril and Sting, and Jim Bowie's mighty blade that bears his name. Missing are the tales of the humble pocket knife. The reason for this is not that the pocket knife is a new invention, but that it is and has always been common. It is the grunt, not the general; a squire not yet knighted. And while it may be through the sword we know many grand tales, it is through the pocket knife that we know the man. The small knives found by archaeologists over the years, just as those passed down in recent generations, are markers of lives lived and work done. In them is a touch of the everyday and a deeper connection to the past than we can experience in their magnanimous counterparts.

IRON AGE TO THE MODERN AGE

Some of the earliest evidence of a foldable knife appeared in Austria and dates back to 600–500 BC, a time when Romans occupied the territory. It seems our ancestors were also not keen on stabbing themselves in the crotch, and thus mother necessity once again gave birth.

I can see it now: Manulus and his Roman compadres are huddled around a fire, shooting the breeze and talking about things such as virtues and Romulus and Remus and how fortunate they were that Romulus was the brother that lived, else they would be called Remans, which just sounds weird. As the throng of men are nodding in agreement that the aqueduct was the swellest thing ever invented and how nothing would ever top it, Manulus, nonchalantly, pulls out his pocket knife, flips it open, and proceeds to cut into a pear. Though he's pretending to look off into the distance, out of the corner of his eye he can see his pals taking notice, and hears a quell in the spirited conversation. One man says what the others are thinking: "Say, Manulus, what's that you have there?" to which Manulus responds, playing dumb, "It's a pear. You've all seen pears, right? Want a slice?"

"No, man, that knife thing you have. Where did you get that?"

"Got it? Oh, no, I made this. Just a little something I worked up this weekend," replies Manulus, to which could be heard the guttural sounds of approval from his eager audience.

As this new folding knife makes its rounds through the host of men, one remarks, "Well, I bet he couldn't make one with a stag horn handle," to which Manulus responds, "By Zeus' whiskers, I bet I can. I'll even polish the steel."

And so the challenge was taken up, and this new version, which was created with an eye toward form as well as function, was received more heartily than the first. At this point, some of Manulus' friends began to feel quite asinine for their previous esteem and admiration of the aqueduct, which seemed to them, now, to be an artless turd river compared to this fine new implement, and they all began placing orders for Manulus' new invention, which he dubbed the Sans Stabby.

While this may not be a truly historical account of how it went down, what we do know is that in the centuries to come, the folding knife is seen everywhere, from the arsenals of Vikings to the pockets of field hands. The style of knives ranged from fancy to formidable, but the basic operation remained true to the original. It isn't until the 1600s, however, that we begin to see a stable design pattern that appealed to the mass of the common man. Enter the peasant knife.

THE PEASANT KNIFE

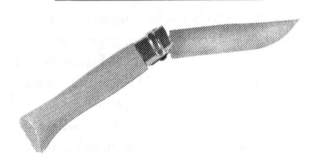

There are a number of things for which we owe the humble peasant a firm handshake and pat on the shoulder. Of course, it would be prudent to immediately shower afterwards, but he has his thanks coming just the same. Without the ages of the struggling lower class, we wouldn't have things such as these:

- Bacon—Once thought of as a cheap cut of meat, now considered food royalty.

- A hearty immune system—Thanks to the Black Plague and generations stewing in their own filth, our bodies have adapted to the otherwise deadly world in which we live.

- Pitch forks and torches—How else is one supposed to run monsters out of the village?

- Bacon—So good, it's worth a second mention!

And, of course, the peasant knife, an affordable friction folder produced in Sheffield, England. It should come as no surprise that it was this unassuming design that became the stolid workmate of many a farmer. Friction folders are a simple design still employed to this day. The snug fit of the blade in the handle is what holds the blade in position. The straightforward design of the knife allowed it to be mass-produced and sold to the common man for a mere English copper, by which the knife got the nickname penny knife, and the rough use of the knife on the farm and in the fields earned it another name, sod buster.

Perhaps the greatest testament to the peasant knife is that it is still a stable sidekick. The French company

Opinel has been making a fine version of the peasant knife since 1890. It's a fantastic folder to keep in the glove box and tool box, plus it still has a classic look that pairs perfectly with camping trips. I suppose other people feel the same, for as of the writing of this book, Opinel sells around 15 million of their knives a year. Peasants everywhere, unite!

The success of the peasant knife and the burgeoning of the Industrial Revolution spawned an advance in knife technology that has scarcely slowed since the mid-1600s. As the Industrial Revolution paved the way for a middle class and afforded them a higher standard of living, the marketplace opened in a way never before seen. In the 1700s, competition amongst inventors of all kinds became fierce as the patent system began in earnest, and knife makers were keen to create and patent new designs for a tool which had been around for a millennium.

THE SLIP JOINT

Not long after the peasant knife appeared on the scene, a truly revolutionary knife design was born: the slip joint. Every man knows this one well, as it is the basis for the familiar style of knives which have dominated the market for several generations. The slip joint is so called because it does not have a true joint, such as a ball and socket, but slides steel on steel. The bottom of the blade, called a tang, rotates against a piece of flexible steel, called a backspring. Rather than having an actual coil spring mechanism, which would weaken over time, the backspring creates pressure. That pressure, along with the shape of the tang, is what causes a traditional pocket knife to "set" in both the half-open and open positions.

As the slip joint came into its own, variations in designs began to spring up. Some came about in response to the need for different blades to accommodate different types of work, but others were made solely for looks. What was once thought to be merely a tool started to become a statement. Just as a man may have an eye toward the aesthetic in his work, he could now afford the same luxury in his everyday tools. The following knives include the most notable designs to come about in the 1900s.

Origin of the Term "Jackknife"

Pocket knives, particularly slip joints, are often referred to as jackknives, but does this term refer to just any pocket knife? And where did the term originate? While there is no definitive origin for the term, it is most likely a colloquialism incorporating the word "jack," which has been used in a host of words over the years. "Jack" is a Middle English term which refers to "any common man" and has been used to describe that which is common—for instance, jackass (an ordinary donkey or Uncle Rob), jackdaw (a small gray-headed crow), jack-of-all-trades, or jacksnipe (a common snipe). The jackknife refers to any larger slip joint knife, typically with two or more blades, and is thought to be used for common work.

THE BARLOW

This is a classic "boy's" knife, if there ever was one. The Barlow is a medium-sized knife with a tear-drop-shaped handle and one or two blades on one end. The original Barlow was made in Sheffield, England—same as the peasant knife, and in around the same decade—by a man named Obidiah Barlow. Within another generation, the Barlow would be made in America, where it would become a staple of any rugged boy's arsenal. George Washington is reported to have received a Barlow knife from his mother as a reward for his obedience. This knife is now on display at the George Washington Masonic National Memorial in Alexandria, Virginia. It doesn't get much more American than that!

THE PEANUT

The peanut is a small pocket knife, shaped like an elongated peanut, but with a slight curve. The knife likely gets its name from its size as much as its shape. The peanut usually has two blades, a clip point and a pen (see pages 62 and 66), but can come with one or three blades. This is an excellent knife for young whittlers, as the small blades lend to small work. Plus, a smaller slip joint is going to be easier to open.

THE CONGRESS

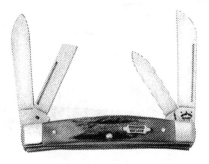

The Congress style of knife is known as a "swayback" as it has a curved body, a concave back, and convex top. When I first learned of the Congress knife, I assumed it got its name because it was spineless. However, it most likely comes from the typical four-blade setup, including a pen blade which was commonly used to sharpen quills. It is reported that Abraham Lincoln carried a Congress knife. Fitting for an outdoorsman-politician, such as he was.

THE STOCKMAN

The stockman is the first knife in this list that was named after work for which it is intended. A stockman is a man who attends to the care of livestock, be it sheep or cattle, and the blades on the stockman are suited to such work. It's a large knife, often shaped like the peanut, with three blades, called the clip, spay, and sheepsfoot.

THE TRAPPER

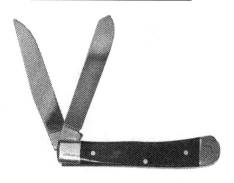

Like the stockman knife, the trapper is so called because it was often used by animal trappers and hunters. The trapper knife has two blades on one end, a clip and a spay. Though the modern design likely originated after fur trading had died down, the name harkens back to older styles of knives, such as the Dog Leg Jack, which had a similar setup and was a popular design among hunters of all types. The longer blade (the clip) is great for sweeping strokes to remove a hide, and the smaller spay is just right for careful cuts, such as opening a cavity. Read more on this topic in the survival section of this book, starting on page 136.

THE CANOE

In my opinion, the canoe knife is one of the finest looking styles. The symmetry of the knife lends credit to its appearance. The body of the knife is shaped like an old Indian canoe and typically consists of two drop point blades, usually a pen and a larger drop point, one on each end. The canoe is a good all-around knife and a particularly good fishing knife. The slightly blunted and broad drop point blade makes quick work of scaling a fish and cutting lines without the worry of an accidental stabbing.

Slip joint knife variations are many, with some styles named after the blade shapes, such as the Elephant's Toenail or the Texas Toothpick, some named after the marketed use of the knife, such as the whittler or the equestrian, and still others named after the shape of the body, as we have seen above. There are varieties of blade configurations within all of these groups as well. A sheepsfoot blade may be swapped for a small Wharncliffe, or a drop point for a spear. Not only can you find a pocket knife styled to your liking, but it makes the world of slip joints a very fun one for collectors as some arrangements are rarer than others.

Surprisingly, many of the classic knife brands are still around, though some in name only. W.R. Case & Sons—better known simply as Case—began selling knives out of the back of a wagon in 1889 and has been producing knives in Pennsylvania since 1905. They are the most widely known and collected of the slip joint brands, and I can personally attest to the quality of their knives. Brands such as Schatt & Morgan and Robeson, which were created by Queen Cutlery (also located in Pennsylvania), have largely disappeared, but

Queen is still in business and makes a classic jackknife that is hard to beat. There has also been an uptick in individual makers of slip joint knives, largely due to the leveling of the marketplace by way of the interwebs and social media. With the marketplace being flooded with cheap alternatives, the desire for one-of-a-kind, handcrafted, high-quality knives has increased.

PENNSYLVANIA AND THE KNIFE INDUSTRY

If you're keen on the history of the knife in the United States, you'll find that most of the early brands hailed from Pennsylvania and many of the companies were offshoots of other established brands. Pennsylvania was, and largely remains, the Hollywood of the knife industry. This should come as no surprise, seeing as how steel manufacturing is so prevalent in the Northeast.

But why did steel settle in that area in the first place? I'm glad you asked. Prior to the turn of the 19th century, steel was created using charcoal. Heaps of timber were slow smoked until charcoal was created. The carbon in the charcoal was used to create steel from iron ore. This, of course, occurred where there was an abundance of timber, which was largely in unsettled areas in North America. New England, however, had been settled and clear cut for some time, so early steel production occurred in iron works located along the waterways where a steady supply of coal could be delivered from the surrounding regions.

However, in the 1800s, coke (a high-carbon fuel derived from coal) replaced charcoal as the preferred means of creating steel. Coal mining areas became a beacon to the steel industry, and as the Industrial Revolution took off, states such as Pennsylvania became synonymous with steel. They also became synonymous with black lung and black skies, but that's a topic for another book. It should be noted that there is still a debate occurring over the quality of steel produced by coke versus charcoal, with many steel enthusiasts claiming that the old method produces a better end product.

THE TRADITION IS ALIVE AND WELL—OR IS IT?

In most cases, when we think about passing down a knife to the next generation, it is a slip joint that comes to mind. They were the knives of our grandparents' generation, and much of this book is devoted to this style of pocket knife. Many of the games and strategies peer back to a time when slip joints were a more common adornment of the pockets of men and boys. But with the advent of locking knives and tactical folders (pages 29 and 35), a question arises: Why a slip joint? What are the advantages of this traditional knife over its modern successors?

There are two things that make the classic slip joint the go-to knife style for handing down. First, they are the kind of knife that much of the tradition has been built around. "But, can't we start a new tradition?" you may ask. For that, I would recommend you see the definition of "tradition." Second, these knives last. They have stood the test of time. Many modern folders (not all, mind you) are made to the standards of a throw-away society and are not built for longevity. It may be that the one you are carrying with you will outlast your days on God's green earth. But, it is also unlikely that it will have undergone the rigors of field-work, hunting, countless honings, and other toils that our forefathers put theirs through.

The slip joint is the knife of the Greatest Generation and the generation before them, and those are some mighty big shoes to fill.

Breaking in a Slip Joint Knife

One of the biggest complaints about slip joint knives is that they are often hard to open when new. If the contact of the tang with the spring is too loose, the blade won't stay open or closed. If it is too tight, you'll break a nail trying to pry it open. At the same time, if the temper (heat treatment) of the backspring is not right, it becomes too stiff. In that case, send the knife back for a replacement if possible, but if not, the only way to break a slip joint in is through repeated openings and closings. Eventually, one of the steels, either the tang or the backspring, will file away, and the knife will be a lifelong companion. Remember, sometimes the best friendships start off rough.

If the slip joint is not opening due to gunk or rust, see the section on maintenance in this book (page 92) for a quick guide on restoring an old pocket knife.

THE SWISS ARMY KNIFE:
One Slip Joint to Rule Them All

"We broke into Mir [Space Station] using a Swiss Army knife. Never leave the planet without one."

—CHRIS HADFIELD, ASTRONAUT,
An Astronaut's Guide to Life on Earth

No pocket knife book would be complete without a strong mention of the Swiss Army knife. While the multibladed, multifunction tool was originally designed for officers in the Swiss Army, it has become a favorite of Boy Scouts and young men, and frequents Christmas stockings and rucksacks like no other.

Even though the Swiss Army knife falls in the same category as the older slip joints in terms of style, it has remained a staple for pocket knife lovers. Perhaps no one is more responsible for keeping the Swiss knife in popular culture as America's most ingenious hero, MacGyver. The mulleted Eagle Scout always had a Swiss Army knife on him, and it seemed to be all that was needed to get him out of any situation. That, and a gum wrapper, or maybe a clothes hanger, along with a good deal of pseudoscience and gumption. In any case, if MacGyver had one, every boy of the mid-1980s wanted to have one.

An interesting bit of history: The official Swiss Army knives are currently manufactured by the company Victorinox. When Victoria, the mother of the original Swiss Army knife inventor, Karl Elsener, died in 1909, he decided to name his newly formed company after her. The particular type of Swiss stainless steel is called "inox," short for "acier inoxydable." The combination of the two words "Victoria" and "inox" is where the company name comes from.

LOCK BLADES

While the slip joint revolutionized the folding knife industry, they suffered from one major flaw that seemed to keep them from playing in the big leagues: They could close on you. Granted, anyone who was familiar with the particulars of a jackknife knew how to use them accordingly, or at least he was made a quick learner. But, for the serious work of skinning and boning, or drilling with the point of the blade, there is real risk of the knife snapping closed, or worse, clamping down on your fingers. To avoid such an ill-fated moment, one need only reach for his lock blade, or fixed blade, knife, and all would be well. And, though a man may like to have an assortment of blades on his person at all times, this is rarely practical. A solution was needed that would allow the beloved and portable folder to get the job done, whatever that job may be. Once the locking blade made its appearance on the scene, however, new designs and innovations soon followed, and pockets and truck glove boxes started getting filled with folders that were as well-equipped for stabbing as they were for slicing.

BUCK KNIVES

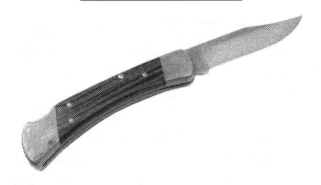

I've mentioned before the elation my young heart felt when I was handed my first pocket knife. It's a sad thing, the human heart, because no sooner was I carving my name into a tree in the woods and whittling my first stabby stick (a stick used to stab things at random—trees, dirt, walls, imaginary foes), than my lustful eyes began to wander to another: my granddaddy's 110 Buck Knife! My little pocket knife was pretty cool, but to me, the Buck is what put meat on the table. Enrobed in ebony, bolstered in brass, a large clip point blade: It was a thing of beauty. And, best of all, it locked! Once I had the basics down with my own slip joint, my granddaddy showed me around the Buck. It was heavy, solid, and sharp, and the familiar "clunk" as the blade set into its opened and locked position gave its owner the sense that this knife was built right, and was made for anything. For us, it did put meat on the table. It was a stable attendant to field dressings and a precursor to many squirrel and dumplings dinners.

As if we didn't owe enough to the "Greatest Generation" America has ever known, we can thank them for one thing more. Born in 1889, Hoyt H. Buck was apprenticed into the art of blacksmithing at age 10. Accounts of his early life show a young man with an adventurous spirit, a hearty work ethic, and a mind looking to improve the everyday implements of life. In short, he was an entrepreneur. At the age of 13, Hoyt was working on heat-treating methods for improving the blade longevity of common tools. It was during this time that the first Buck knife was made, though not the locking folder the company is so famous for now. When WWII hit Pearl Harbor, and the United States decided to hit back, the government declared a dire need for fixed blade knives for the troops and issued a call to the common man for war supplies. Hoyt, a US Navy veteran and now a pastor, heeded the call and set up a blacksmith shop in the basement of his church.

"I didn't have any knives, but I sure knew how to make them,"[1] he said. The fixed blade "Bucks" earned a reputation for being dependable and holding an edge on the hardest testing grounds imaginable. After WWII, Hoyt had a backlog of orders from GIs who could vouch for the brand, even if it was from word of mouth only. Hoyt had taken care of the troops, now they were going to take care of him.

Soon Hoyt was joined by his son Al, and in 1947 they set up a proper shop, H.H. Buck & Son. At first, Al was a reluctant partner, but within a year his father was diagnosed with cancer. Al realized how important the business was to his dad and he began to work tirelessly to master the skills his father had developed over a

---

1   "The History of the 99-Year-Old Buck Knife." *Popular Mechanics*. June, 2001. http://www.popularmechanics.com/outdoors/adventures/1277451.html?page=2.

lifetime. "I can't tell you how many blades I ruined in the process, but finally I was ready," Al said. Once he had the tempering and grinding process down, Hoyt smiled and said, "Now I almost feel my life is complete—my son can make knives!"[2]

Hoyt Buck died in 1949, and Al took the helm. However, it wasn't until 1964 that the now-infamous Buck 110 Folding Hunter, with the locking blade, was born. It was an immediate success. Within six months, Buck knives had gone from a mom-and-pop operation to an industry leader.

THE LOCKBACK

Buck's locking mechanism is so simple it's hard to understand why it wasn't created sooner. Like a slip joint knife, the Buck still uses a backspring, but on the Buck, the backspring fits into a notch on the tang when the blade is in the fully open position (think mortise and tenon if you're a woodworker). Rather than being fixed to the handle, the backspring pivots on a fulcrum and has constant tension from another backspring in

2 Ibid.

the base of the knife handle. To close the knife, you just have to press on the exposed backspring near the rear bolster (the brass ends on a Buck), which unseats the backspring from the notch in the tang.

The Buck company never patented its invention, but they became so well-known for the design it was likely unnecessary. While many others would copy the lock-back, Buck is still widely regarded as the original and the best. Still, Buck's 110 became so popular it showed a clear opportunity for the pocket knife market, and before long new knife designs with locking blades began to spring up (pun intended.)

THE TACTICAL FOLDER

The Gulf War of the 1990s introduced a generation not only to foreign combat, but also to a new kind of soldier. He was sleeker, more efficient, and technically superior to his enemies. Even his rifle rounds had changed from "bigger is better" to "light is right." And, rather than the heavy fixed blades of his forebears, the modern soldier carried a lightweight folder. Originally referred to as a combat folder, these knives quickly assumed the moniker of tactical folder. While they have many designs and opening and locking mechanisms, they typically have similar features: the ability to open with one hand, often by a flick of the thumb (using a thumb stud, a larger opening, or spring assist); a locking blade; and the ability to unlock and close with one hand. The latter feature, one-handed unlocking and closing, was an obvious and much desired feature that many pocket knife enthusiasts longed for. While the switchblade (page 41) and butterfly knives provided this functionality, they were either banned or too large to fit the needs of the everyday Joe-Jack.

Though tactical folders started to gain popularity in the early 1990s, their most notable locking mechanism was invented a decade earlier by jeweler turned knifemaker, Michael Walker. His Linerlock was a revolutionary boon to a new age of knifemakers. Like many of its predecessors, the locking liner is surprisingly simple yet extremely effective. A lightweight strip of titanium alloy or steel is attached to the inner walls of a knife handle where the blade rests. The bottom half of the metal is secured to the handle, while the top puts constant pressure on the side of the tang (think leaf-spring if you're a car guy), reminiscent of the friction folding design from Penny Knives. The pressure on the tang provides just enough tension on the blade to prevent it from flopping open. Opening the blade fully allows the locking liner to pop into place, fitting just under the tang. A push of the thumb to the side of the inner liner releases the lock, and the blade can be closed with the forefinger or a quick slide against your side. Walker's official Linerlock design employs a ball detent to keep the blade closed as well.

Though Walker developed his Linerlock shortly after entering the knifemaking market in 1981, the design was limited to his own knives until other knife-making enthusiasts picked up on the artistry and simplicity of the design at knife fairs.

Much like the slip joint knifemakers of the 1800s, those of the late 1980s and '90s were open and influential on each other's designs, which aided in the progression toward the modern tactical folder. We see a web of new folders based on Walker's Linerlock and his early knife designs, and many now-familiar brands were inspired to start in those early days. One such maker is Ernest Emerson, who credits seeing Walker's knives at a knife show with his inspiration to forge ahead with his own aspirations.

While the Linerlock is the mechanism by which so many tactical folders get their style, Emerson's tactical folders are where they got their mettle. In the mid-1980s, elite Navy SEAL team members requested the creation of a lightweight folder from a well-known knifemaker, Phill Hartsfield. Hartsfield was known among the SEALs for his fixed blade knives, but he didn't make a folder and so referred them to Emerson. Emerson was the perfect fit. Having begun his knife-making endeavors crafting a butterfly knife (also called a balisong) for a Filipino martial arts class he was taking—at his kitchen table, no less—Emerson had a long history with knives used in tactical scenarios. Living in Southern California and working in the aircraft industry provided him access to rare, light-weight metals. Emerson's tanto-tipped CQC-6 (Close Quarters Combat SEAL Team 6) tactical folder was a hit amongst the SEALs, and gave credence to the light, quick, and compact tactical folder as a sure and gutsy blade for the modern soldier. Where the slip joints and penny knives had been tested in the fields of farmland, the tactical folder had now been tested on the field of combat.

Tactical or Tacticool?

In the last few decades, the tactical folder has dominated the knife market. The demand for these folders has been so great that the marketplace has been flooded with cheap alternatives to this hardier knife, which is meant to do real work. In contrast to the simple design of the slip joints, the tacticals have largely been made to satisfy the desire to carry something that looks cool, regardless of the quality. The result is what you would imagine: many a blade rusting away in a landfill rather than holding a place of honor in one's sock drawer or cabinet of mementos.

The fault lies not with the tactical folder, as its SEAL-worthiness has already been attested to. Rather, it rests with greed, and a move away from simplicity in design. Lesser quality folders of all kinds replace properly tempered steel components for screws and springs that are hardly above aluminum foil in durability. In order to compete in such a market, even the well-known brands have made cheap versions of otherwise quality blades. So, how is one to avoid being so easily duped into purchasing a pocket knife that is more "tacticool" than tactical? The old rule of "you get what you pay for" still applies here. Stick with the brands that have a history for dependability, lean toward the higher-end knives, and steer clear of the bargains.

SWITCHBLADES

What knife book would be complete without at least an honorable mention of the switchblade? Certainly not this one. Before tactical knives hit the scene, the switchblade satisfied most of the major elements which made the knives so popular, and did so half a century earlier. Switchblades flick open with the push of a button, lock into place, and can be unlocked with a single hand. However, the blade is designed for pointed operations such as a stab to the heart, not carving or serious strikes. These shortcomings could have been easily overcome. Unfortunately, this gentleman's knife was given a bad reputation before it had a chance to shine.

At the end of World War II, GIs returned home with Italian "stiletto" switchblades. (Leave it to the Italians to design a knife that was meant to kill you, but looked so darn cool that you had to bring one home and show it off.) Before long, the knives were being imported from Italy, but by the 1950s, they had become associated with America's misguided youth. The stiletto knife was portrayed in movies as a favorite of greasers looking for trouble—so, of course, if you were a greasy-headed punk, you had to have one. I personally think many of the actions by boys during that time was an attempt at finding the toughness in manhood so manifestly displayed by their fathers—even, and especially, the fallen ones.

At any rate, the knife gained popularity and prominence as being more flashy than useful, and in the mid-1950s, US politicians began a platform of criminalizing the possession and carry of the quick steel. Typically, the criminalization of dangerous things makes those things seem more cool and desirable, particularly amongst those who also believe breaking the law is cool, thus increasing the coolness and want of said illegal item. It's no wonder, then, that regardless of whether or not the switchblade was ever a true rebel's rapier, it was doomed to be classified as a tool of terror by the law. As of the writing of this book, the switchblade and other automatic knives of its ilk vary in their legality. Each state here in the US has differing laws, some outlawing possession and carry, others having rather stupid laws which allow possession and open carry. I mean, really? Are you going to hang it around your neck or something? Perhaps there is a market for t-shirts saying, "I has a switchblade" which is both informative and funny, as it will allow fearful types to keep their distance, and also drive grammarians mad.

Why a Stiletto?

The term "stiletto" is often synonymous with the popular Italian switchblade, but it actually hails from medieval times. The original stiletto was a fixed blade weapon favored by knights. Similar to the switchblade, the ancient stiletto had a needle-nosed blade and was used primarily as a thrusting weapon, often to finish off a wounded foe as a "mercy strike." With enough force, the pointed blade could penetrate chainmail and slip past plates of armor to deliver an iron thorn to the heart. The switchblade was designed primarily as a thrusting knife, and as such, it was given the moniker of stiletto.

Other automatic knives in the switchblade family have come under similar scrutiny. The Out to Front (OTF) is perhaps a less familiar design, but it's nonetheless worthy of mention. Rather than the blade flipping open from the side, it thrusts forward, out of the front of the handle (hence the name; we men try to keep things simple). While the single action OTF requires the wielder to manually reset the blade back into its hidden and closed position, usually via an exposed lever, the double actions pop out and in with the press of a button—think Wolverine's claws, but in your pocket. *Snikt!*

ODE TO THE SWITCHBLADE

Some may speculate that the switchblade did not take a seat of prominence due to the myriad of legal issues and overall questionable views of those who possessed one. This is a solid theory, but I have another. I believe the switchblade was publicly executed.

In 1986, an image of the Land Down Under and the indelible mark of a man who found confidence in himself was forever impressed upon the minds of many Americans, and likely the world. Mick Dundee was a staggering contrast to the effeminized men of the '80s (save Ronald Reagan, of course) and boys, speaking from my own experience, took to heart his ways. I am, of course, speaking of Crocodile Dundee. Dundee, along with Indiana Jones and a handful of others, displayed a rugged self-reliance and determinism that had been all but abandoned since the days of Cowboys and Indians. I firmly believe it was Crocodile Dundee who unknowingly staged an execution of this fanciful blade we call the stiletto. So great was his influence on the minds of the young that the switchblade would, for a generation or two, be thought of as cool, but not "Dundee" approved.

I have, not very befittingly, written a poem, or perhaps a sardonic eulogy, for the infamous scene in which the act took place.

You lost the war, but our soldiers brought you home.

The boys, when they saw you, thought
you were bad to the bone.

Pulled from a pocket, glistening steel,

Italian design, but nonetheless real.

With the press of the button, your lightning blade shone.

Awe was struck in all men, be they boys, be they grown.

The gub'ment wasn't for you; they had
your number, had your name.

Being the knife of rabble-rousers
was the height of your fame.

Outcast and restricted, you pressed on through the years.

The sons whose pockets you filled, were
their mother's worst fears.

Till one day in Brooklyn, where you met your match,

The man from the outback, was
the wrong man to attack.

He leapt from the shadows, ready to strike,

But instead of a toothpick, he should
have brought a knife.

With the flick of his wrist, you certainly looked cool,

But to threaten Dundee's sheila,
takes a special kind of fool.

He cut him to ribbons, in true Aussie style.

In turn you fled, for in his pants was a pile.

My mate said it once, but I'll say it again

"That's not a knife," but this is my friend!

I will admit that the Dundee effect may only last a generation or two, but it has nonetheless placed this admirable blade in an unflattering light. However, the scene may also have served to reset public opinion surrounding this estimable skiver and allow it to once again enter the pocket knife community, on equal grounds with its latter cousins.

THE 9/11 EFFECT ON KNIVES

The events of 9/11 and the increases in terrorism have placed any and all items which could be viewed as dangerous under the spotlight. Once a common boyhood possession, the trusty pocket knife is now viewed as an implement of terror. Questions such as, "Why would a man need to carry a knife?" are answered by "Only if he wants to kill innocent people!" This is the mindset of many, divorced from the practical and honest intentions of the pocket knife.

Yet, there has also been the call to "be alert" and "be vigilant," both of which prompt a man to be ready, reminding him that this world is not yet tamed. It is ironic that the events that cause some to be afraid of violence are the same ones that embolden others to readiness and strengthen resolve. In many ways, the threat of domestic terrorism has legitimized the tactical folder as the standard-bearer of everyday carry. Whereas the slip joints meet the needs of the farmhand and fisherman, the tactical folder symbolizes the great need of the age: for men to be ready. Granted, a knife of any kind is of little good in a shooting or bombing, but that's why I say "symbolizes." Along with its practical purposes, a knife reflects a people and a time.

Regardless of the knife you choose to carry, or if you have several knives for different uses, there is no doubt that the common view of this age-old implement has undergone a change. The public display of a knife, even for opening a box, can be a bit of a shock to some. If you find this is the case, a great way to get more people comfortable with a knife is to let them use it. Mistrust often comes from ignorance. Once someone has an opportunity to use a pocket knife and realizes it is not going to jump into their eye-socket or make them stab people, they feel knowledgeable and empowered. So, instead of just whipping out your blade like a badass, think about your audience, and use the moment to instruct.

BUYING A KNIFE

Recent generations have about them the idea that products of all kinds are, by nature, transitory. In other words, things are not supposed to last and are therefore made cheap so as to be easily replaced. Whereas this line of reasoning would have been sacrilege to the makers of old—and still is to the quality makers of our age—it pervades the conscience of the consumer. You may find that a high-quality tactical folder will cost $100 or more, which may seem outrageous, as there are plenty of $40 and under models available. Yet, when you consider that this knife will accompany you every day, serve in countless chores, and time and again display both its wear and readiness for the job, it's quite the deal. And, when you consider that it will one day be a treasured item handed down to your children (and possibly their children), it becomes, in a sense, priceless.

This isn't to say there is no place for the lesser quality models; there certainly is. A man ought to have a glove-box knife, a fishing knife (that will no doubt stink to high hell), a toolbox knife (well-oiled and chipped), camping knives, and so forth. I think that a hunting or skinning knife should be of the highest quality, even if it is rather specialized for the task, but there are many occasions where a throwaway knife isn't such a bad thing to have on hand—particularly in the case of the fishing knife. If an investment can be made to purchase a quality blade in each area of use, all the better, but the one that should take a place of prominence is your everyday carry. Learn more about how to choose the right knife in Chapter 4.

CHAPTER 2

KNOW-HOW

"Fill your bowl to the brim and it will spill. Keep sharpening your knife and it will blunt."

—Lao Tzu

There are few things more embarrassing than handing a man (or a boy old enough to know better) a knife, and seeing them test the sharpness of the blade by running their finger down the length of the blade. I can probably come up with a few things more embarrassing, actually. Let's see…men figure skating, wearing capris, looking on helplessly as other men change his tire, calling his wife "the boss," and drinking skim milk. (You can thank Ron Swanson for that last one.)

The goal of this chapter is to imbue you with a depth of knowledge that will not only keep you from slicing open your finger, but also allow you to hone a knife well enough to make a clean cut, should the errant attempt be made. Knowing your way around a knife of any kind is important, and much of what you learn here will be of value regardless of knife type. However, the pocket knife has additional points (see what I did there?!) that, when learned, will make you something of a blade scholar and appreciator of all things knife.

While the fascination with bladed things seems to get passed down to men genetically (and unlike male pattern baldness, men are glad to have it), the particulars of bladesmanship are not, and must be passed down intentionally. The best way for this to occur is one on one, father or grandfather to son. Some of the things that are discussed in this chapter are nuanced, and watching and getting a feel for them yourself is the greatest way to learn. A patient instructor will not only give direction, but also encouragement in the effort, and so the passing on of knowledge is a heartfelt, bonding experience as well as a cerebral one. Dads,

I highly recommend you read this chapter then walk your kids through it, rather than just handing them the book.

Regardless of whether you are a dad or an uncle or just a regular bloke, this chapter contains the know-how to get you up to speed on handling, sharpening, cleaning, and understanding your pocket knife.

TESTING YOUR METAL

Before jumping into the well of knifery know-how, here is a little quiz to determine your current standing on the subject. The answers are at the end of the chapter (no peeking).

1. This type of blade is great for cutting twine and pruning.

    A. Drop Point

    B. Shear

    C. Hawksbill

2. One of the best stones for honing a knife blade hails from this state.

    A. Ohio

    B. Arkansas

    C. New Mexico

3. Texturing a bone knife handle to give it the appearance of antler is known as.

    A. Jigging

    B. Strafing

    C. Antlerizing

4. True or False: A clip point blade is ideal for puncturing tough materials.

    A. True

    B. False

5. The metal junction between a knife blade and its handle is called a:

A. Joint

B. Bolster

C. Pinstay

6. The part of a blade that extends through the handle is called the:

A. Hilt

B. Splay

C. Tang

7. This type of knife blade does not have a belly.

A. Sheepsfoot

B. Straightback

C. Tanto

8. A person who carves images into bone (commonly knife handles) using a pointed tool is called a:

    A. Sailor

    B. Scrimshander

    C. Shawman

9. True or False: When passing an open knife, you should hold onto the handle.

    A. True

    B. False

10. Which of the following is NOT a locking mechanism for pocket knives?

    A. Lockback

    B. Axis Lock

    C. Inline Lock

    D. Frame Lock

Bonus: If you should find yourself in prison and were to shape out a knife-like implement that may be used for slicing or stabbing, said implement would be called a:

A. Shiv

B. Shank

KNOW YOUR BLADES

Understanding the types of blades commonly found in knives, the work they were intended to do, and the pros and cons of their design is like base camp in the ascension of knife know-how. Much like the designs of the slip joint knives, blades are often named either for their appearance or their utilitarian purposes. The spey blade, for example, is so called because it was used by herdsmen to spay their livestock. The clip point, on the other hand, is so named because it looks like the last third of the blade has been "clipped" so that the tip sweeps upward to a point. While there are many blade types, the nomenclature associated with them makes for easy remembrance and recognition.

Before we get down to business, let's make sure you have the basics down.

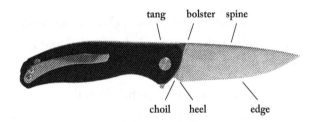

Spine. The back, unsharpened edge of the blade. The thickness of the spine creates a strong knife and is generally tempered to be softer than the blade (especially true on larger knives). This allows for the blade steel to flex rather than snap.

Edge. The sharpened, "cutty" part. Blades can have two edges, such as double-edged sword or spear points. Blades can also have a false edge, which is usually a ground, but not sharpened, spine. Blade edges should be tempered to be harder. This allows a blade to sharpen and hold its edge. However, tempering the edge correctly is challenging; too hard an edge can become brittle and chip. The right blade will hold its edge and not easily chip. *Note:* Blades that have a curved edge are said to have a "belly," whereas straight-edged blades do not.

Heel. The lower part of a blade, close to the handle. Larger pocket knives have may have a heel, but most simply have a choil.

Bolster. On a larger knife, the bolster is the unsharpened portion of a blade which sits between the blade and the handle. On a pocket knife, it is often a decorative metal end which serves to cover up the pivot point of the blade. The Buck 110 folder has the classic brass bolsters on the top and bottom of the knife handle. In any case, bolsters are often used as an area of decorative distinction between brands.

Choil. A notch between the edge of the blade and the tang. It serves as a marker for the end of the cutting edge.

Tang. The part of the blade which attaches to the handle. As pocket knives are folders, the tang is usually quite short. In fixed blade knives a "full tang" knife is always preferable, as it means the tang runs the length of the handle.

The following is a listing of some of the more common blade designs. Note that when it comes to blades, there are many variations on a theme. The clip point, for example, has a number of members in its family, including the trailing point, which has a longer "clip" and blade. There are Turkish-styled clip points which sweep upward, reminiscent of a scimitar. However, understanding the basic designs and their strengths and weaknesses makes it easier to recognize the blade and its purpose, no matter the final shape.

CLIP POINT

One of the most popular blade shapes, the clip point is so called because the last third or so of the blade is "clipped," creating a sweeping tip of the blade. By reducing the spine (and thus the width of the tip), the blade excels in quick penetrations on softer surfaces, like a bear abdomen. It should be no wonder that this design has been seen since the Stone Age and made its way onto Jim Bowie's famous blade. For pocket knives and smaller blades, the recess of the clipped point acts like a cradle for the forefinger, with the finger, then, acting as a governor for the depth of the blade penetration. This is particularly helpful when skinning or field dressing an animal as it is often necessary to control the blade depth, quickly and efficiently.

DROP POINT

The drop point is another popular blade shape. Where the clip point is concave, the drop point is convex. In most cases, the drop point spine is only slightly tapered compared to the edge, hence it "drops off" at the tip. The forward edge of the spine is often ground to a false edge to reduce drag on entry. Because of the heftier spine, the drop point is preferred for thrust that needs to be more accurate. The clip point design causes the blade to enter quickly, but it moves off target. For practical purposes, the drop point is also a safer design due to the tip being less pointed (as long as you're not trying to kill something, that is).

SPEAR POINT

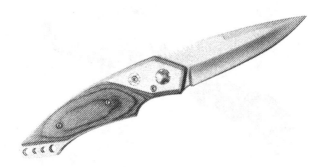

Spear points differ from drop points in that the spine of the blade mirrors that of the edge, thus having a very symmetrical shape like that on ancient spears. A spear point blade may have a dull spine, half sharp spine, or double edge, though the point is most effective when the blade is double-edged.

SPEY

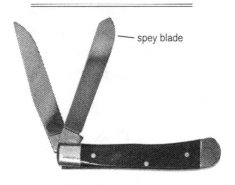

spey blade

Most commonly found on the trapper and stockman slip joint knives, the spey blade is a bit of a misnomer. Though it was used by trappers for skinning and stockmen for castrating, the spey blade was not likely used for spaying. However, this is easily explained. The word "spay," which we use to refer to female sterilization (neutering for males), comes from the Greek word *spathe*, which means "broad blade." The use of the term was interchangeable in reference to the work of castrating, and thus a blade which was good for castration could also be called a "spay" blade.

What makes this blade ideal for skinning and castrating is the dull point. Unlike the sheepsfoot, which still has a point where the spine meets the edge, the spey has a very dull and ineffective point, which helps to ensure there are no unintentional nicks during the castration.

PEN

This is a small spear-shaped blade originally used for trimming quills. The pen blade is found in a variety of slip joint knife designs, including the Congress and the peanut styles.

SHEEPSFOOT

This blade is so named because of its prevalent use in trimming sheeps' hooves. The blade edge is straight while the spine curves down to meet the edge of the blade, creating a blunt tip. You will see blunt tips on knives that are intended to be used in close quarters, where an accidental stabbing may be likely. (I'm not a shepherd, but I believe stabbing the sheep you are caring for is looked down upon.) This blade type is also ideal for shaving large swathes of wood, so it's a favorite of whittlers.

COPING

The coping blade is much like the sheepsfoot but its spine meets the edge at an angle, creating a bit of a point. Like the other straight-edged blades of its ilk, the coping is great for whittling. It has also been a favorite of electricians, carpenters, and all-around handymen.

WHARNCLIFFE

Though the exact origins of the Wharncliffe blade shape are unknown, it has long been a favorite of sailors. Like the sheepsfoot, the Wharncliffe has a straight edge, but its spine meets the edge at a sharp point. This makes it ideal for whittling and puncturing. This blade has the advantages of an awl and making shavings fly.

TANTO

The tanto is a Japanese inspired blade design with a chisel-like point, a mostly straight edge, and a hefty spine. The point of the knife is angled rather than having a sweeping belly, which creates a very solid tip that is perfect for puncturing hard materials without breaking, making this the perfect blade design for stabbing through Kevlar, should the need arise. Tanto blades are generally hardier and thicker than others, which, despite their elegant design, makes them handy for grunt work. Not to be confused with Tonto, the Lone Ranger's sidekick.

HAWKSBILL

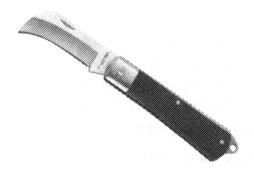

Curved like the beak of a bird of prey, the hawksbill is a great farmers' knife. It's fine for grabbing and cutting slippery twine, as well as pruning plants. Bellied knives tend to slip against a surface, and thus rely on their honed edges to cut. A hawksbill has the advantage of cupping an object, allowing maximum pressure to be applied without the blade sliding unwarranted.

HOW TO PASS A KNIFE

When instructing someone in the ways of knifesmanship, one of the first lessons which will be taught is how to pass an open knife to another person. This is especially important if your pupil is a youngster, as they tend to flail the blade about, forgetting they are wielding a stabbing and slicing apparatus.

Now, you will no doubt hear people, including professionals, say that you should never pass an open knife. If it is a fixed blade, sheath it; if it is a foldable, close it. I think that advice is pretty stupid. It's a great way of saying, "I am about to hand you a potentially dangerous item, but let's be clear that I don't trust you to take it from me without cutting one of us." This is similar to the notion, "Don't hand someone a loaded gun." How about this instead: Don't hand knives (or guns) to people you don't trust to have some common sense about them. Sometimes it is necessary, or simply convenient, to hand someone an open blade, and since you are going to do it anyhow, you should make sure you do it the right way.

There are a few accepted ways to hand someone a knife. I'll list three that come to mind, but the main point is to not hand someone…well, the point. Never hand an open knife to someone with the point facing them. Not only does it cause the person to whom you are passing the knife to question the thin veil of friendship and sanity that lies between the two of you, possibly putting them on the defensive, but it's also impractical and unnecessarily dangerous. Should you attempt to pass a knife point-first to a trained ninja, you may find yourself receiving a swift and impulsive kick to the groin before either of you knows what happened. Assuming you would like to one day conceive children, avoid this scenario by following one of the rules for the safe tender of a knife.

THE SWIVEL:
Handle Between Forefinger and Thumb

The most efficient and optimal means of passing an open knife to another person is to swivel the knife by the handle, from between the forefinger and thumb. To do this, start by holding the knife in standard fashion.

Loosen the grip on the knife handle except for the forefinger and thumb, and swivel the knife backward so that the spine of the knife is touching the webbing between the finger and thumb, and the handle is facing the person you are handing the knife to.

This method is optimal, provided you have a single-edged or false-edged knife. For double-edged knives this is problematic, because rather than the spine of the blade resting on your skin, it will be a sharpened edge. When the person takes the knife from you, there is a chance they will cut the webbing between your forefinger and thumb. There is a rumor that pianist Robert Schumann purposely cut the webbing between his fingers to get a better reach on the piano, and while this may be an area where a friend and sharp knife can help you out, it is unlikely the intent when passing a knife. In any case, if you're concerned about your webbing, there are two other means by which to pass a blade that will work for any knife.

THE PINCH:
Blade Between Forefinger and Thumb

Provided the knife isn't going to be used for food preparation, this method works well with any blade type. Simply hold the knife with the blade facing you, firmly grasped near the point by your thumb and the crook of your forefinger.

The main drawback to this method is that oil passes from your fingers to the blade. Not only does it leave prints on a mirror finish, but oil will also erode the steel (see our bit on maintenance on page 92). Don't be offended if the receiver of the knife promptly wipes the blade off on his shirt.

THE OFFERING:
Across the Palm

Of the methods used to pass an open knife safely, I like this one the least. There is something about having an open knife resting in my palm that doesn't sit well with me, though it is effective and straightforward. Simply lay the open knife horizontally across your palm with the blade and handle facing outward. Offer the knife to the person, allowing them to pick it up by the handle.

The drawback to this method is that the knife is not secure until the receiver has purchase of it. This could result in the knife being dropped, but the chances are pretty slim. You can increase the comfort level in the exchange by holding your thumb on the handle to secure the knife. This, of course, increases the risk of getting cut by a double-edged knife, but hey, life is not without risks.

PASSING A KNIFE BACK

There is an oft forgotten, yet gentlemanly rule for passing a knife back to its owner: When possible, clean and close the knife before passing it back. Assuming you are done with the knife, clean it with your shirt or pocket handkerchief (yet another good reason to always wear flannel, as it both cleans well and hides stains…not like you needed a reason, though), close the knife, and give a solid "thanks" to its owner. A "much appreciated" can also work, but you may also throw in a "boy, that's a sharp knife," which says it all, and pays the highest compliment.

Practice the knife-passing behaviors suggested above and you'll get plenty of knife-karma points in your favor, making it far more unlikely that a knife will ever fall upon your toes or cut through a major artery. It also shows that you know what you're about and take the business of knife handling seriously.

TOOLS FOR HONING A BLADE

The sharpness (or dullness) of a man's knife can provide valuable insight into his character, at least in terms of his relationship to and appreciation of his tools. Any man who has been handed a pocket knife and subtly tested its sharpness was, at the same time, silently passing judgment upon its caretaker. The verdict of that blade test would either uphold, elevate, or demote the knife's owner in some vaguely defined yet serious way; the quality of a man's blade affects the way he is regarded by other men. Admittedly, this can be a challenge, as pocket knives are generally used for grunt work, which quickly dulls the blade and for which a very sharp blade is often not required. If you should find yourself in such a position where your grunt blade is being inspected, it is best to readily admit the neglect of the edge before you are found out. This may not save you face, but the only thing worse than feeling the edgeless blade of a friend's daily carry is a friend that never considered it.

In any case, the best way to avoid a dull edge is to hone your blade. I can still remember my granddaddy sharpening his knives in the den of our small country home. In many cases, this would be before or after a hunt. The TV would be on, and we would watch *Wheel of Fortune* or some show, while in the background could be heard the *shhhhh, shhhhh* of the blade against the stone. Proud of himself, he would pass the knife to me and I would test it for an edge, which it certainly had.

Let's be clear: Getting a knife decently sharp is not hard. The basic process involves scraping steel across the face of a flat rock with a bit of oil or water. While there are better "rocks" available for purchase these days, the process hasn't changed much throughout the centuries. These tools can be purchased at a reasonable price, and cheaper alternatives will get the job done as well. However, the tools that you cannot acquire from a store, but are nonetheless indispensable for the task, are patience and savvy, both of which come about through trial and error.

These are terms that a blade-toting man should be familiar with.

Whet—Meaning "to sharpen." Not to be confused with "wet," as these words have nothing to do with one another. You can't sharpen water.

Grit—A method of determining particles per square inch. The higher the grit, the more particles per square inch. Higher grit removes less material, ultimately resulting in a polished finish. Grit also refers to perseverance in a man. In either case, a man should have a good deal of grit if he wants to hone his blade or himself.

Swarf—The bits of metal debris resulting from the honing process. Nothing clever needed here; the word is funny on its own.

WHETSTONES

The first step in honing your blade is to select a quality whetstone. The classic setup, at least in Western cultures, includes an Arkansas oilstone, a bit of honing oil (traditionally neatsfoot or sperm whale oil, but the hippies have made sure you'll have a hard time finding the latter), and a rag. Newer and credible alternatives have come on the scene, and ancient Eastern methods of sharpening have become mainstream, as well.

As the names suggest, each stone type is associated with the necessary lubricant to carry away the swarf: oil for oilstones and water for waterstones.

Waterstones have been used for centuries by Japanese swordsmiths to hone their blades, and they take honing very, very seriously. A culture that was honor bound to hara-kiri (ritual suicide by disembowelment) can be trusted to fine-tune the art of sharpening blades.

Waterstones work either by being immersed in water, in which the stone absorbs the water, or, for very fine stones which have a denser grit, water is used on top of the stones. Being more porous than oilstones, waterstones are subject to wear and occasionally have to be flattened with another stone. However, waterstones are superb at getting a high-polish finish to your blade.

Natural oilstones, such as Arkansas stones, require the use of oil on top of the stone to carry away the swarf. They have the advantage of being harder than waterstones, and thus can last for generations. India oilstones are a man-made alternative to the Arkansas stone. Created by Norton, a trusted brand for sharpening systems, India stones are made of aluminum oxide. They function much like an Arkansas stone in that they require oil, but they remove material more quickly. They are sometimes used in conjunction with a hard Arkansas stone to finish the edge.

DIAMOND PLATES

Yes, friends, you can now sharpen your blades with diamond dust. As the name would suggest, diamond plates have fine particles of diamond on the surface and can be used with oil or water alike. While they break from the tradition of stoning (using a stone to sharpen a blade), they are quickly becoming a favorite. Diamond plates are great for honing, especially if you are sharpening a very dull blade, as they remove material very quickly.

So, what's the drawback? They just don't feel right. Don't get me wrong, they are capable, and I use them for sharpening chisels and the blades of my hand planes (plane iron) for woodworking, but they just don't have the weight and the spirit of a waterstone or oilstone. That being said, they are great for putting an edge on a knife, and if that is what you're after, then you can't go wrong.

CERAMICS

When we think of ceramics, we typically think of delicate objects, or maybe toilets (hey, we're guys!), but we probably don't consider ceramic for sharpening steel. However, certain types of ceramics are several times harder than stainless steel and are ideal for quickly putting an edge on a blade.

The most popular ceramic option for knife sharpening is a set of ceramic rods manufactured by Lansky. These rods are set into a base and extend vertically at an angle. The blade is drawn downward on the rod, as if it's trying to slice through the rod. The result is the blade scraping the rod at a preset angle, usually 20° or 25°, and a quick edge is put on the knife. The nice thing about these ceramic rod systems is that they do not require oil and can be packed away easily. Plus, the various angles make it dead simple for sharpening knives of all types. They typically come with medium and fine grit rods, so you've got most of what you need out of the box.

Honing Oil

While you're not likely to find sperm whale oil, neatsfoot is still available, though it's not necessarily the best option. Neatsfoot, by the way, is made from the oil of cow shin bones and feet. I'm questioning how "neat" that really is, but you have to admire people for making use of a cow shin.

Honing oil will be available wherever you happen to procure your stone or your knife. All of the big-name knife manufacturers have their brand of honing oil. The main consideration when choosing an oil is to make sure you use a non-drying oil. Vegetable oils or tree-based oils will eventually dry and clog the pores of the stone. A great non-drying oil for honing is Hoppe's gun oil. Not only will it work for your knives and your guns, but it's excellent at removing rust and lubricating the knife—plus, it smells super manly.

SHARPENING A KNIFE

The key to putting a razor-sharp edge on a knife is having a good sharpening setup that goes from a medium to very fine grit, and understanding the angle at which a knife should be sharpened is essential. Each blade has an angle, and sharpening to that angle will yield the best result.

KNIFE BLADE ANGLES

Understanding blade angles is important but not complicated. Lower angles of 15° or less are going to be sharper than higher angles. This may lead you to think that a pocket knife with a 5° bevel is what we're shooting for when honing a knife, but hold on just a minute. The lower angles are not only sharper, they are more brittle, and they are intended to cut softer materials. A 10° blade would be excellent for a filleting knife, but not so great for an all-around jackknife. An axe, for example, may have an angle of 35°, but then again, some guys like their axes sharp enough for shaving.

Pocket knife blade angles usually range anywhere from 15° to 25°. The thinner the blade, the smaller the angle. If you aren't able to determine the exact angle of your blade, not to worry; you can get a feel for the right angle when sharpening.

PUTTING AN EDGE ON IT

Start by oiling or watering your stone as necessary. To get a feel for the angle of your blade, place the knife blade flat on the stone and slowly begin to rotate it toward the edge. In most cases, you will be able to feel when the blade flattens on its edge, meaning the angle of the edge is now parallel with the stone. If you have a well-used blade or one with a nick, you'll want to go slightly past this angle so that you're carving into the stone. So, for example, if your blade is parallel at 20°, you might want to adjust to 23°. This will result in more material removal from the knife blade. Once the edge is free of nicks, you can drop back down to the proper angle.

The sharpening is done by pushing the blade toward the stone as if trying to slightly cut the stone. Unlike rod-based sharpeners, which are meant to put a quick edge on a blade and can be used very quickly, stones will remove more material and should be used slowly. If the blade has an edge on both sides, be sure to use the same number of strokes on each side so that you maintain symmetry.

Move from the lower grit to the higher grit, noticing how each successive stone puts a polish on the edge.

FINISHING OFF WITH A STROP

Though not necessary, a leather strop certainly puts the final polish on a blade, removing the burs and giving a truly razor-sharp edge.

Leather strops come in different grits as well, but typically you'll want the finest grit and use it as the last step. A strop kit will contain the strop, which is a hunk of leather on a wooden block, and some polishing compound. The compound looks a bit like a crayon mixed with chalk. Rub the compound on the strop, just enough to give it some color. As the strop is more for buffing than for material removal, you're going to draw the knife blade in the opposite direction across the strop than the direction you used when sharpening. The goal is to remove the burs and put a mirror finish on the edge.

HOW TO TEST A KNIFE FOR SHARPNESS

When someone hands you a knife, the first instinct is to test it for sharpness. This not only gives you an indication of the readiness of the knife for the task, but also makes a statement about its owner. However, when sharpening your own knife, there are a few steps to testing the sharpness to ensure you have the finest edge possible.

The thumb. The quickest way to test a knife for sharpness is to run your thumb across the blade, perpendicular to the edge. Do not run your finger lengthwise along the blade, as this will cut you, resulting in bleeding, ruined clothes, a bloody knife, and your looking like a moron.

Three fingers along the edge. While it is not a good idea to mindlessly run one finger along the edge of the blade, mindfully running more than one finger along the edge of the blade can be a good way to test for sharpness. To perform this test, hold your first three fingers side by side and slowly, gently move them along the edge of the blade. A sharp blade will begin to cut through the fingerprints on the finger and your brain will let you know when you've gone too far—hence the "mindfully" part of this test. Using very light pressure, this technique can be helpful to discover burs along the edge.

Paper cutting test. Grab a sheet of paper—magazine pages are great for this. Starting from the heel of the knife, cut the paper with one stroke, moving to the tip of the knife. Feel and listen to the paper as the knife is cutting through. Does it catch at any point? How well does it slide through the paper? Typically, the heel and the tip will be the areas that need some extra attention when sharpening, as they are the hardest parts to effectively press onto a stone, but the paper cutting test will also reveal any burs or nicks in the blade.

Hair shaving test. Once a blade has a mirror edge, it should be able to cut hair. This is the ultimate test of knife sharpness. Holding the blade nearly flat on the skin of the arm, give short shaving motions across the hairs. You should not feel a pulling sensation, but rather a smooth shave, and you should see the hairs piling on the blade.

WHY IS MY BLADE NOT SHARP?

There are a few reasons that a blade may not have an edge even after taking it through the sharpening process.

Your angle is not right. If the angle is too great, the blade will not be very sharp.

The edge is folded over. If the blade edge becomes too thin, the steel may not be able to handle it and the edge will roll over. You can usually feel this with a simple thumb test, but poor-quality steels can be problematic, as the rolled edge shifts from side to side. If this is the case, you'll likely need to sharpen at a higher angle or upgrade your blade.

You're dulling the edge with inconsistent angles. When sharpening the knife, if your angles are not consistent between stones or when switching sides, you may be inadvertently dulling the edge instead of sharpening it. The finer grit stones will polish the blade edge and reveal more of the angle. Be sure that the entire edge is being sharpened, not just the very edge of the edge.

POCKET KNIFE MAINTENANCE

Along with the responsibility of keeping a blade sharp comes keeping a pocket knife in good working order. Perhaps you have inherited an old pocket knife that isn't what it used to be, or you've neglected the care of you own. With a little TLC and know-how, a pocket knife can be restored, and usually without taking it apart.

STEP 1: CLEANING THE BLADE(S)

It may come as a surprise to many, but even stainless steel can rust. Even a day or two of neglect after the blade has been wet or touched can lead to corrosion. I have seen some steel rust along the very outline of the fingerprints that touched it. While this is unfortunate for the owner of the knife, it makes sleuthing out the guilty party all the more easy and vengeance can be exacted—this being in the form of having them clean your knife, not stabbing them, lest there be any confusion.

In any account, a blade which has some rust or grime can be brought back to life fairly easily using one of these methods.

Green scrubbing pads and honing oil. Scotch-Brite makes these little green scrubbing pads, and they are just excellent for cleaning the rust off a blade. Simply apply a bit of honing oil or gun oil to the blade, and scrub away. The goal is to remove the rust without scratching the blade, which is why these pads are preferred.

If you have a stubborn spot, grab some 1000-grit or higher sandpaper and do the same. If you're looking to restore a shine to a blade, finish with sandpaper at finer grits, say 1500, 2000, 2500...all the way to 8000. A polishing compound can also be used, but unless the knife really calls for it, a bit of wear actually looks good.

Stab a potato. Potatoes contain oxalic acid, which is good for dissolving rust, and it's fun to stab things, so this method is win-win...unless you're a potato. Simply stab the blade into the potato and leave it for a few hours. Take the blade out, rinse it with water, and dry. Then, bury the potato near the neighbor's mailbox or fence. Sharing is caring.

Soak the blade in white vinegar. Vinegar contains acetic acid, which is also good for dissolving rust. Come to think of it, acid is pretty good at dissolving all kinds of things, so it's best not to put the entire knife in the solution. This method will likely take half a day or more to work, but it can get the job done. Be sure to rinse the knife off well and dry thoroughly.

Baking soda scrub. Baking soda not only works as a deodorant, a makeshift toothpaste, and a culinary must-have, it can also be used to clean a number of items. I can't believe we actually eat this stuff. Anyhow, a bit of water, some baking soda, and a paper towel makes a good recipe for cleaning a rusty blade. The drawback to this method is that the baking soda paste can get into hard-to-reach places of the knife if you're not careful. Stick to the blade and you'll be set. Wash and dry when done. Excess baking soda can be thrown into the vinegar from the previous suggestion for a little science-class fun.

STEP 2: CLEANING EVERYTHING ELSE

Once your blade is nice and spiffy, the rest of the pocket knife will look more dingy. However, with the application of time and water, everything can be cleaned.

Thawing a frozen blade. If you have a knife that has rusted shut, you can probably free it up by spraying it with WD-40. What am I saying? This is a *Guy's Guide to Pocket Knives*! You most *certainly* can free it up with WD-40! I once heard a story about the CIA interrogating a terrorist. They tried all of the typical techniques to get him to talk, but nothing was working. Then the janitor came in the room, sprayed the guy with a bit of WD-40, and everything came spilling out. Two weeks later, we took out bin Laden. Coincidence? Conspiracy? Clever marketing? Completely untrue? I'll let you be the judge.

Getting the grime. Most older pocket knives cannot be taken apart, so getting into the hard-to-reach places requires a few common household items: a toothbrush,

Q-tips, toothpicks, and a paperclip. The paperclip is great for getting deep into the handle and digging out the gunk. The other items are pretty self-explanatory. With some honing oil or WD-40, you can spiff up an old pocket knife in no time.

STEP 3: KEEPING IT CLEAN

The last step in pocket knife maintenance is to not let it get grimy in the first place. After use, wipe the blade on your shirttail and close it by touching only the spine of the blade, or fold it closed by pressing it against your clothes rather than your hand.

When sharpening the knife, allow a bit of clean oil to get in the joints, but be sure to wipe away any oil contaminated with swarf. It's not a bad idea to run a newly sharpened knife under water, then thoroughly dry it and add a small amount of honing oil.

TESTING YOUR METAL ANSWERS

1. C

2. B

3. A

4. B (A clip point is good for puncturing softer materials.)

5. B

6. C

7. A (A sheepsfoot has a straight edge and no belly. A tanto has a slight curve to the edge.)

8. B

9. B

10. C

Bonus: A—Shiv. The word Shiv comes from ancient Romani people and is simply another word for knife; having both a point and an edge. Shank is an old English term which correlates to stabbing, thus having a point only.

CHAPTER 3

CLASSIC GAMES AND PASTIMES

"There was never a good knife made of bad steel."

—BENJAMIN FRANKLIN

It seems there is a point in each generation when they are gripped with nostalgia, and the memory of their younger days, and even that of their parents, becomes gilded. Times were tougher, and people were stronger, better looking, and of course, had more common sense than the foolhardy generations that came afterward. As I embark upon my forties, I can feel this setting in for myself as well, and it may be nostalgia talking, but I do believe there is some truth to it.

There are things that existed in my generation that would never be invented now. Take, for instance, the in-car cigarette lighter. For those not familiar with this device, let me explain how it worked. There was a device in your car that you could press into the console, and after about 10 seconds or so, it became so hot that it glowed orange. You would then take this glowing hot device in one hand and light a cigarette that you held between your lips, effectively lighting a small fire stick held in your mouth, all whilst traveling at interstate speeds and navigating corners and whatnot. Those things were great; everyone loved them, and there was absolutely no protection for kids, or from accidentally dropping them between your legs and setting your groin ablaze. The disappearance of these kinds of things does not justify labeling the next generation as "soft," but the fact that they would never be created because they are considered "too dangerous" kind of speaks for itself.

Pocket knife games likely fit into this category, as well. Only a few lifetimes ago, boys were left to spend hours playing games that involved tossing multi-bladed knives into the air and allowing them to fall where they may, sometimes to see how close they could come to a boy's foot without being hit. That these classic games have been displaced by modern pastimes is not surprising, but that they would be deemed dangerous in the eyes of today's parents speaks of the great need for them.

MUMBLEY-PEG

Also referred to as Mumblety-Peg, Root the Peg, and other similar variations, Mumbley-Peg is the most classic of the classics when it comes to pocket knife games. It should be noted that the name Mumbley-Peg has been attributed to all sorts of knife games, including some of those mentioned later in this chapter. So, there is a chance that what one person remembers as Mumbley-Peg is vastly different from another person's version. In any case, this is the most common description of the game and seems to fit well with the name.

The game works a bit like the basketball game H-O-R-S-E, with players inventing trick shots, except that the sequence of increasingly challenging knife throws and sticks are set before the game begins.

An example of Mumbley-Peg game play may look like this:

Throw #1: Standing straight with feet together, hold the knife by the tip between your forefinger and thumb of your right hand, and bring the handle to touch your nose. Flip the knife forward so that it sticks in the ground. Repeat with your left hand.

Throw #2: Standing as before and holding the knife between the forefinger and thumb of your right hand, cross your arms so that your left hand has hold of your right earlobe and the knife handle touches your left ear. Toss the knife to your left or over your left shoulder and stick it in the ground. Repeat with the left hand.

Throw #3: Balance the opened knife tip on the thumb of your right hand, using your left hand to steady it. Flip the knife into the air and stick it in the ground.

Repeat for all fingers and then switch to the other hand.

Throw #4: Kneeling down on both knees, hold the knife by the tip between your forefinger and thumb of your right hand, toss the knife over your head and behind you, and stick it in the ground. Repeat with your left hand.

Throw #5: After the last stick, pop the knife with your right hand so that it flips out of the ground, makes a few rotations, and sticks in the ground again.

These steps can be done individually, so one boy may beat the rest of the pack by completing the steps first, or they can be done in turn. The winner(s) will drive a small peg nearly flush with the ground using his pocket knife. The loser has to get the peg out with his teeth, hence the mumbling and peg.

MAMA PIG

I first came across Mama Pig in Marcus Brotherton's excellent book *We Who Are Alive and Remain: Untold*

Stories from the Band of Brothers. It was Corporal Dewitt Lowrey (1922–2015) who mentions this game, and it sounds easy and fun to play.

To play Mama Pig, you need an old Barlow knife with three blades. Open the two largest blades all the way, and the shortest blade only halfway, 45°, to the handle. Place the shortest blade in the ground so that the two largest blades point outward. Using a stick under the blade or your finger under the handle, flip the knife up so that it rotates. The goal is to get the largest blade to stick in the ground. What does this have to do with a mother pig? I have no idea.

CHICKEN

Depending on how brave or stupid your friends are, a game of chicken can end pretty badly. However, it's a good way to push your fears and possibly earn some cool scars.

Chicken is played with two people and one or two pocket knives; any single blade that can be thrown and stuck in the ground will work, and typically, a boy or man will want to use his own.

Start off standing across from one another, with your legs shoulder-width apart. Player #1 will throw his pocket knife between the feet of Player #2. If it sticks in the ground, Player #2 will move whichever foot is closest to where the knife struck to the location of the knife, thereby decreasing the width of his stance. If the knife did not stick, no foot movement is necessary.

Player #2 will then throw the knife between the feet of Player #1. This back and forth continues until the agreed upon number of "sticks" (the sticking of the knife into the ground between the feet) has been reached, or until one of the  players becomes too afraid of getting his foot impaled and calls "Chicken," thus becoming the loser.

What happens if you get stabbed in the foot? There are finer details of this game to be worked out on a play-by-play basis, but typically, any stabbings would result in an immediate shift to a new game called, "Don't tell your mom!" All boys who didn't want to be forever branded as a "Chicken" would certainly keep their mouths shut.

SPLIT THE KIPPER (OR STRETCH)

Whereas Chicken is a game of ever moving the feet inward, Split the Kipper, commonly known as Stretch, is a game of moving outward; essentially, it's the reverse of Chicken.

To begin, two players stand facing one another with their feet together. Player #1 throws his knife to the side of one of Player #2's feet, and Player #2 moves his foot to touch the knife. Player #2 then throws the knife to the side of one of Player #1's feet, and thus both players begin to spread their feet further and further apart. While there is an element of Chicken here, since throwing a knife at an angle increases the risk, the real challenge is staying on your feet. The opponent that topples over first loses.

Note to self: Never play this game against Jean-Claude Van Damme.

BASEBALL

In lieu of a sunny day and a real bat and ball, a pocket knife version of this classic American pastime can be played indoors or out, but it works best when you have an old table or bench. Sailors would play this game on the wooden deck of their ships.

To play pocket knife baseball, you'll need two players and at least one two-bladed pocket knife, with two blades at one end, such as with a Barlow or peanut knife. Open the smallest blade (often a pen blade) fully, but the larger blade (often a clip point) only halfway, so that the blades are jacked, forming a 90° angle.

To start the game (at the home plate), loosely stick the point of the larger blade into a board so that the knife handle is facing you and the smaller blade is pointing away from you. Flip the knife up and over with your finger under the handle. The knife should rotate and come back down. How the knife sticks the landing will count as a foul, an out, or base hit.

- Lands on its side—Out

- Lands on its back with the blades pointing up—Foul

- Small blade sticks with no other blade touching—Home run!

- Both blades touching the board—Three-base hit

- Large blade sticks in the board—Two-base hit

- Large blade sticks with handle touching—One-base hit

The game is played like baseball, with three outs per turn for nine innings.

PROPERTY (OR LAND)

The game I have heard called Property has gone by several names, such as Land, War, Sea Battle, and even Mumbley Peg. The goal of the game is to seize as much of another person's space as possible, until they have no more room to stand.

To play Property, you'll need two players, each with their own knife, though I suppose you could get by with just one pocket knife. One player will draw a large circle, big enough for both players to stand in and still have a bit of room. A line is drawn down the middle of the circle, creating a half for each player.

Player #1, chosen randomly by flipping a coin, rock-paper-scissors, or display of knife skills, will toss their knife into Player #2's half of the circle so as to stick it in the ground. An imaginary divider will be formed based on where the knife lands and the direction the blade is pointing. Player #2 will draw a new line in the direction of his opponent's blade, reducing his own share of the space. The old line will be erased to show his opponent having a larger share. Player #2 can only stand within his space.

Player #2 will throw a knife in turn, thus dividing his opponent's area and increasing his own. A player gets an advantage when his opponent's throw fails to stick.

As you can imagine, this game can go on for some time, with two people going around in an ever-changing circle. The game ends when one player has no room to stand, steps out of the circle, or bows out, afraid of being hit by the knife.

Note: This game can be played outside of the circle as well. Simply make the circle smaller to begin with, divide it, and play the game like normal. The game is finished when one player is only left with a space of a predefined width, like the handle length of a pocket knife.

WHITTLING
AND CARVING

Whittling is likely the commonest of ways to pass the time with a knife of any kind. Many a boy has sat on the porch piling up shavings just to have something to do, the end result being a mess of shavings and a pointy stick. There is something satisfying about forming a long, smooth cut of the bark from a green limb. But whittling can be serious, delicate business as well. A true woodcarver may have several knives that work better for different angles and various sized pieces, and when tackling a fun project, he may have them all open and switch from one to another. A common whittler may have one pocket knife and not worry so much about refining the final piece, or may focus on less intricate projects such as a spinning top or a slingshot.

In any case, with a sharp knife and a bit of soft wood, an afternoon of quiet reflection and handcraftiness can be had.

THE BASICS

Getting started with whittling is like getting started with most good adventures in life. You need a few basic things: a sharp knife and a positive attitude. Oh, and you also need some wood and an idea, but those are readily available on most whittling afternoons where time is also plentiful. Of course, selecting the right wood and knife for the project will greatly aid in the enjoyment of the process.

CHOOSING THE RIGHT POCKET KNIFE

A whittling knife generally needs to meet these requirements: It must be sharp, have a good straight edge on a blade, have a good tip, and be easy to hold and maneuver for the task.

A small peanut knife can work just fine, provided you are whittling something small. A stockman will also work well for something larger. Many knife makers have knives tailored specifically to the whittler, such as Case's Seahorse Whittler, which has a Wharncliffe blade and usually a few smaller blades, depending on the configuration of the knife.

Drop points and spear point blades are not usually preferred for whittling because they lack a long, straight edge. They tend to slice at an angle, slipping along the wood, when controlled strokes are often critical.

CHOOSING THE RIGHT WOOD

Woods are typically classified as hardwoods and softwoods, but not all hard or softwoods are the same. Woods like cherry can be considered a hard or softwood, and maple comes in both hard and soft varieties. Furthermore, grain becomes important when carving a piece of wood. Woods with strong grain direction will be harder to carve because the knife will want to follow the direction of the grain. Softwoods with a lot of knots, such as pine, can be problematic for whittling, plus they will have a good deal of sap if they are freshly cut. Sap is not a whittler's friend.

If you're making something without a lot of detail, a soft wood such as maple (red, sugar, or silver) will work just fine. Birch and aspen are also fine woods for whittling. If making something such as a slingshot, where only minimal removal of wood is needed, it doesn't really matter what type of wood you use, so long as it is strong enough for the task at hand.

For smaller, more detailed pieces, basswood is the best you can find. Basswood is a light, plain-colored wood with a very tight grain pattern, so it doesn't fight the carver or force him to go with the grain.

Whether you're looking for basswood or some variety of maple, you will most likely need to go to a professional woodworking store or order online, as these woods are not sold in most box stores. If you have this wood available locally you can use it, provided it has dried out indoors for a period of time, generally six months to a year. Green wood (undried) can also be used, but the final piece may crack after it dries. Keep in mind that as you work your way closer to the core of the tree, the wood becomes harder.

CARVING TECHNIQUES

Practice with carving wood is going to teach you far more than a book's description, but there are a few techniques that are useful for beginners.

Pushing with the thumb. Whittling smaller pieces requires more control than with larger ones, and the pressure of the blade into the wood grain needs to be consistent and careful. The wood gives feedback to the whittler, and the whittler needs to respond by giving more or less pressure. Holding the knife firmly and pressing on the back of the blade with the thumb (rather than with the wrist) helps control the blade and allows for smaller movements.

Pulling toward the thumb. While cutting toward oneself is generally discouraged, it is often necessary when carving wood. This technique is employed when peeling an apple. The knife is held in the hand with the four main fingers, and the thumb acts as a brace for the object, allowing the knife to be drawn through the apple or wood.

Chip carving. In order to carve out a section of wood, the chip carving technique can be used. This is helpful when you don't want to cut too much wood, which is important seeing as you can't easily put it back.

The first step in chip carving is to score a line where you want the end of the chip to be. A straight-edged blade with a sharp point is great for this—think coping or Wharncliffe. Simply press down with the blade into the wood, or draw the line with the tip of the blade. More than one scoring line can be created to further control how much wood will be removed.

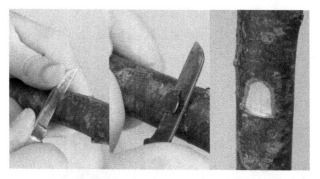

The second step is carving out the chip. Here, the blade of choice depends on the shape of the wood and the chip being removed. A sheepsfoot blade can be useful, as it has features which lend themselves to controlled work. Care must be taken to not cut past the scoring line. The blade is used as a chisel, and the scoring line provides a pre-cut marker allowing the cut to be defined.

Much of carving is moving around the wood with constant chip carving; thus, some forethought must be given to each cut before it occurs. It's not uncommon to see a man turning his bit of wood over a few times, looking at it like a Rubik's cube, deciding the next few moves.

CARVING PROJECT 1: MAKE A SOAPALLO

No greater mammal has graced the North American frontier than the mighty buffalo, also known as the American bison. Carving the likeness of this grand beast from a bar of soap is the perfect project for a beginner, as it will imbue the student with many of the techniques of carving without the frustrations (and potential dangers) of carving a block of timber.

Why are we using soap? Well, every red-blooded man knows soap has no practical value, save as a bitter reminder for boys not to say swears in front of their mom. Buffalo, on the other hand, have many practical uses: They taste good, their coarse wool makes fine clothing, they fertilize the land, their heads look really cool mounted on a pub wall, and, I may be thinking of some other animal here, but I am pretty sure they like to give people rides. More than any of these, the American bison is a symbol to behold; a wonder of God's creation. To be fair, I suppose you could eat those hippie soaps made from coffee and oats and hemp or whatnot, but you can't grill it or serve it as jerky, and marijuana soap is not America's official mammal...at least not yet.

The point is, soap is boring and terrible. It's your job to turn it into something cool.

WHAT YOU WILL NEED

The tools of choice are a pocket knife, preferably one with smaller blades, and a bar of soap. A pencil or other pointed object will also come in handy for outlining your bison. Any brand of soap may work, but some of the cheaper stuff crumbles, so you'll probably want to stick with the name brands that have a good bit of moisturizing qualities.

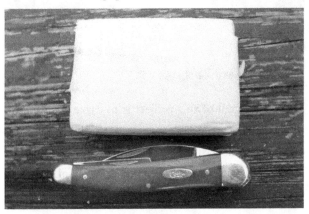

For this project, I am using a Seahorse Whittler by Case. As the name suggests, it's an excellent pocket knife for whittling/carving. It has a large Wharncliffe blade, perfect for cutting long, straight swaths of wood (or soap), along with a small coping blade and pen blade.

Step 1: Draw an Outline of Your Buffalo

The initial goal of this project is to carve a silhouette of the buffalo, so it's best to draw the basic shape of the creature on the soap before you begin. Unless you have a photographic memory, look up a picture of a buffalo on the interwebs for inspiration and proportioning.

Step 2: Carve the Basic Shape

The second step is to use your pocket knife to carve out the shape of your buffalo. In some cases, you will need to cut with a swipe of the blade, and in others you will need to notch a piece out. Depending on the soap you've chosen to use, you may or may not be able to put pieces back, should you take off too much.

Step 3: Turn the Silhouette Into a Statuette

Before starting this step, it's a good idea to take your silhouette to someone else and ask them what animal you are making. If they say it is some kind of humped-back dog, you may want to start over. However, should they say, "A bear?" you're close enough and may proceed.

Now comes the hard part. An artistic eye and patience is necessary to turn your soap into a statuette. Here are a few pointers:

• Bison are wider at the head and shoulders than at the hips

- Bison legs appear relatively short in comparison to the rest of their frame

- The face is shaped like a heart, wider at the top and narrowing at the chin

Step 4: Enjoy!

If your Soapallo turned out really well, it's a good idea to give it as a gift to your wife or girlfriend or one of your kids. If it turned out not-so-great, not all hope is lost. Simply make a soap Plains Indian, a soap Cowboy, and maybe some soap tumbleweed. Take them all to the bathtub and pretend that the Soapallo was a recent kill and that Cowboy and Indian are celebrating a successful hunt and newly formed friendship.

CARVING PROJECT 2: WOOD SPOON

Hand-carved treenware—wooden cutlery, dishes, and bowls—are a fantastic way to show off your skills with a knife, knowledge about woods, and creativity. Each piece is unique, having character all its own. A wooden spoon stands out in particular, because the concave end causes people to wonder how it was carved.

While there are knives made especially for spoon carving, we are going to accomplish this with just a pocket knife.

WHAT YOU WILL NEED

Anytime you are working with wood that will come in contact with food, you want to use food-safe woods and non-toxic oils to seal them. A good rule of thumb is to stick with fruit and nut trees, such as apple, pear, plum, walnut, pecan, etc. Keep in mind that those with nut allergies may also have a reaction to nut woods such as walnut. For this example, I am using a bit of plum wood from one of my trees.

The diameter of wood should be around 2 inches to make a good-sized spoon, and about 5 to 6 inches long. You will also need a sharp pocket knife. For this project I used my drop point half-serrated Leatherman c33x. It has been a trusty little knife, and the serrations are actually good for carving.

Step 1: Mark the Center Line

We want to use the roundness of the stick to work as the underside of our spoon. Mark a line across the center of your stick, as shown in the illustration. It may be helpful to mark the belly of the spoon as well, just to get an idea of the potential depth of the spoon.

Step 2: Split the Wood in Half

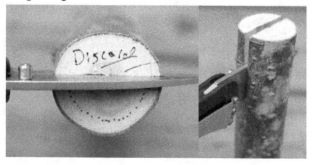

Using your pocket knife as a wedge and another stick as a hammer, pound the pocket knife into and down the stick, lengthwise. As long as the grain is running straight, you should get an even split. If the wood has some twists in it, that's OK. It adds to the character of the final piece.

Step 3: Outline the Spoon Shape

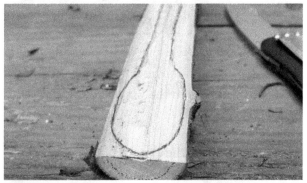

Using a pencil or pen, or by scoring the wood with your knife, make a rough outline of the desired spoon shape.

Step 4: Whittle Away Everything That Is Not a Spoon

The goal here is to create a spoon silhouette, but not to get too detailed with the design just yet. Carving the bowl may put stress on the wood, and we don't want the handle to snap off.

Step 5: Carve Out the Bowl

Even with a spoon-carving knife, this step is tricky, so it's even harder with a pocket knife. Start by scoring the inner edge of the bowl. Then press inward and at an angle with the tip of your knife. This helps establish a barrier and helps prevent shaving off wood you don't mean to.

The carving of the bowl is done by scoring the perimeter of the bowl, with lines going perpendicular to each other, so that the inside of the spoon looks like a checkerboard. Then, using just the tip of your knife, press and peel away each square. Do this successively until the bowl of the spoon is carved away.

Step 6: Whittle Away the Excess

Continue whittling away the remainder of the stick until you have a spoon. The most common mistake new spoon-makers make is having too deep or too thick of a spoon bowl. Spoon bowls are typically narrower at the tip and deeper near the handle. In order for it to be comfortable to use, the spoon bowl needs to be fairly thin.

Step 7: Sand, Apply a Finish, and Enjoy!

Sanding your spoon will be necessary to both make it look like a finished product and prevent splinters. In the wild you can use a coarse grit rock to accomplish this, but at home, good old sandpaper works. Using something with around 320 grit should get the job done.

Treenware needs to be protected with oils. If you happen to be in the woods, it doesn't really matter because you can just make a new spoon, but if you want to give it away or use it for meals, oil will not only protect the spoon from the accumulation of germs, but it also brings out the grain and colorations of the wood better than any soup can do. Any salad bowl oil, walnut oil (careful with allergies), linseed oil (raw, not boiled), or mineral oil will work. Other oils, such as tung oil, can be used, but they may have a bitter taste or off-putting smell.

SCRIMSHAW

In the days of the weather-worn sailor, men of the sea entertained themselves in the manly and creative pastime of scrimshaw. Much like whittling, the salty men of old would etch drawings into whale ivory and stain those etchings with tobacco juice or ink to bring them to life. As the explorers of the seas became pioneers of the American frontier, they brought the tradition with them and adapted it to work on antler- and cow-boned knife handles. Not only was this a way to pass the time, but it also worked to brand the knife, as men would often use their initials or simply etch an image that was unmistakably theirs. Scrimshaw has made a comeback, and while whalebone is not going to be as easy to find, there are substitute materials that work just as whale. (See what I did there?)

A great way to get started with scrimshaw work is to get a pocket knife scrimshaw kit from Mollyjogger (Mollyjogger.com). Not only does the kit come with a stabilized cow bone pocket knife, but it also has a number of nifty designs that have the right kind of old-school feel and fit. However you go about scrimshaw work, here are the steps you will need to take to have your art turn out right.

You will need the following supplies:

- A pocket knife with a stabilized bone or imitation ivory handle

- Beeswax, if not using a stabilized or sealed material

- A pointed tool, such as a steel dental toothpick

- Ink or dark stain

- Q-tips

- Transfer paper (optional)

- Magnifying glass (optional)

BEFORE YOU BEGIN

If using an unsealed surface, rub beeswax thoroughly into it to seal the pores. Otherwise, the ink will stain the entire surface and not just the portion you have etched.

STEPS TO SCRIMSHAW

The hardest part about scrimshaw work is deciding on the design. If you are new to the craft and unsure of your artistic abilities, it's best to start with something easy, unless you have a design to trace and follow. A whale is a classic symbol of the sea, and although it's a bit ironic to carve a whale onto a whalebone, perhaps it could be viewed as a tribute of sorts. Simple designs can most likely be done freehand, occasionally applying ink to reveal the etched design. More complex designs may need the aid of transfer paper and tracing of the image onto the flat surface of the knife handle. In any case, etching with the sharp tool is how you will get the design engraved onto the knife handle.

1. If necessary, trace the design onto the knife handle using transfer paper.

2. Using your pointed tool, scratch the basic outline of the design into the surface of the knife handle.

3. Apply ink to the surface using the Q-tips and wipe away. This should reveal the etched area.

4. Continue until the image is complete.

There are techniques used in line drawings that can also be applied to scrimshaw work to add depth to your image. Cross hatching is a technique of making hashes (#) to represent shadowing. Stippling is a method of using dots at various intervals to simulate a gradient effect as well. The closer the dots or hashes, the darker the shadow effect. With scrimshaw work, hashes are typically easier to etch than dots, but take your time and see which works best for you.

Pro tip: Having a magnifying glass on a flexible arm is a great advantage when doing detailed scrimshaw work. The small gradation in waves of the sea or curves of a lighthouse can make the difference between something cool and a very impressive bit of scrimshaw handiwork.

CHAPTER 4

SURVIVAL & TACTICAL

"War to the knife, and knife to the hilt!"

—NATHAN BEDFORD FORREST

If you knew you were going to be stranded on an island or out in the wilderness and could only bring one item with you, most men would say a knife is the item they would bring. A knife, even a small pocket knife, is an indispensable tool for survival. Yet, you don't have to be on a deserted island to find yourself in need of a knife to save your life. The scenarios in which a well-honed blade could save a life are endless, and we'll cover a few of them in this chapter. Chances are that if you do find yourself in a difficult or life-threatening situation, it won't be one of the ones covered in this chapter, but one rule remains constant regardless of what life throws at you: Be prepared.

SELECTING THE RIGHT POCKET KNIFE FOR SURVIVAL

When we think of pocket knives of old, they were largely chosen based on the work that was being done on a daily basis. A man would see a knife and think, "that would be just about right for doing thus and so," and would carry that knife around, accomplishing tasks with a great deal of pride. When we think of a survival pocket knife, much of the decision in what knife to choose comes down to the work that may need to be done, rather than the familiar everyday work. This means taking into account the likely scenarios one might encounter in a survival situation and thinking about how a pocket knife might be used to accomplish the tasks. Here are a few questions that will help you frame the decision-making process.

- Where will the survival scenario take place? In an urban or wilderness environment?

- How long are you expecting to survive?

- What will be this knife's responsibility in the building of shelter?

- How about in the gathering or hunting of food?

- Will it be necessary to use this knife in a fight with a man, or bear, or a really large, hairy bear-man?

Once you have a picture of the survival scenario in your mind, you can begin choosing the knife, or knives, for the task. Regardless of which knife you decide to go with, there is one quality which every knife must meet.

DURABILITY

For all of the scenarios that you've envisioned, there is one thing you'll definitely overlook, unless you already have the experience: It will be harder than you imagined. It will be more aggravating that you can know from the comfort of your couch, dreaming up scenarios in which you play the hero. The necessity for a knife that works correctly will be paramount. Therefore, durability is the number one characteristic a knife must have for you to even consider buying it. This doesn't mean believing clever marketing; rather, it means choosing a knife that has a lifetime or more of worthwhile testimony to its hardiness. A pocket knife with billions of features isn't worth a dern if it falls apart, or the blade snaps, or if most of those features are not key to survival.

Your survival pocket knife must perform, time and again, under very rough conditions. Name brands are not always a marker of quality, so you'll have to do your research before making a selection. Look for articles and videos on field test results of knifes. Most cheaper knives will show wear in a short period of time when put to more severe tests. While the big brands do have good knives, they are often not the ones you will find on sale in a box store. A high-quality, durable knife that may one day save your life will stand out from the crowd.

Here are some questions to be answered when looking for a dependable pocket knife.

- How long does the blade stay sharp?

- Does the edge or tip chip easily?

- How well does the knife withstand impact, such as being dropped or thrown?

- Is the knife assembled with screws or pins (pins being preferable)?

- How reliable is the locking mechanism?

- Is the knife corrosion resistant?

STEEL SELECTION: STAINLESS OR CARBON?

The quest for the golden ratio of carbon and iron has not yet ended, and blade enthusiasts will continue to make their cases for what types of steel are the choicest. For survival, it's not necessary to go into extreme detail, but understanding the pros and cons of stainless and carbon steel blades is important.

Note: All steel has carbon, but when we talk about carbon steel, we're talking about a type of steel that uses a higher amount of carbon as the alloying ingredient during production. An alloy is a substance with metallic properties formed from two or more elements; the alloying element in steel can give it certain characteristics like hardness or rust resistance. Stainless steel uses chromium as the main alloying ingredient, because chromium is inert and aids in corrosion prevention.

Stainless steel is less brittle than carbon steel. A stainless steel blade will bend before it breaks, whereas a carbon steel blade is more likely to snap. Stainless steel also resists rust better than carbon steel, though there are coatings on many newer blades that make them fairly rust resistant. Carbon steel, on the other hand, holds an edge longer than stainless steel. This harder edge is great for making clean cuts time after time, but comes at the cost of being more brittle and more easily chipped.

Keep in mind that all carbon steels are not the same, and blade steel will have other elements mixed in to create the right balance of all the great features a blade should have. Once again, time-tested durability will be the best measure for any blade.

BLADE FEATURES

While MacGyver preferred his Swiss Army knife to a heftier single blade, that may not be the best choice for every survival scenario. Plus, let's just be honest here, there is only one MacGyver, and only he could really pull something like that off. So as long as you're not MacGyver, take the time to account for the features that a survival pocket knife should have before making a selection.

SIZE MATTERS

Considering the best pocket knife is the one you have on you, it makes sense to select a knife that is both easy to carry (not too large), as well as handy on a daily basis. Unless you know you are packing out into dangerous territory, you will most likely find yourself needing a pocket knife when you least expect it. While the larger blades and knife are appealing and useful, if the size of the knife becomes a hindrance for daily carry, it's best to leave it in the truck, tackle box, or backpack and select a pocket knife of reasonable size to have on your person.

SERRATED EDGES

A serrated edge is pretty darn handy when cutting rope and vine. Whereas a straight-edged blade will slip along a wet vine, a serrated edge is more likely to saw through. Most pocket knives will have a combination serrated-plain edge, making for the best of both worlds. The plain edge is generally for whittling and skinning, which the upper half of the blade is typically used for anyway, leaving the lower half of the blade serrated and useful for heavier duty cuts.

What about sharpening a serrated edge, you ask? In most cases, there is no need. One of the benefits to a serrated edge is that they remain useful much longer than plain edges do. Though the points on a serration can chip or become dull, their lifespan is still greater than that of plain edge.

MULTIPLE BLADES, OR JUST ONE?

Much of this question comes down to the type of knife you want to carry. A modern tactical folder is going to have one blade and a pocket clip. A classic slip joint can have more than one blade, but without the pocket clip. Having more blades means that they will be smaller. However, there is still an advantage to having several blades: More edges can mean having a sharp blade available for a longer period of time, and the blades can be specialized to different tasks.

Another important factor to keep in mind is the necessity of a strong locking mechanism. Most multi-bladed knives forgo this in favor of the convenience of blade choice. Unless the configuration of blade types is extremely useful, it is best to stick with a strong single blade that has a proven lock.

EXTRA FEATURES

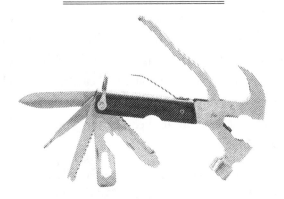

Marketplace competition being what it is, new features have been added to modern knives that are pretty cool, but are questionable in their necessity. Whether it is a seatbelt cutter, a glass breaker, or a bottle opener, these features should be of secondary consideration in light of the main points already mentioned. If you should find yourself in a precarious position, the chances of needing a specialized feature are much slimmer than those of needing a good, all-around pocket knife.

PUTTING YOUR KNIFE TO USE

A knife is only as good as the man who knows how to use it. There are basic survival skills that, sadly, have been lost to the generations that grew up with 24-hour grocery stores and Starbucks. Actually, Starbucks doesn't have much to do with it, I just wanted to get at least one jab at them in this book. Mission accomplished.

The following scenarios are a perfect place to use a pocket knife for survival, and they can all be tested in your backyard.

THE FIGURE-4
DEADFALL TRAP

The deadfall is a simple trap designed to bludgeon or pin a small animal. While they are easy to make, they can be tricky to set up. The trigger mechanism is brilliant in its simplicity, and just like a mouse trap, you want it to be stable except when confronted with the right amount of movement. Then, *pop*, the animal is dead or caught, and starvation is not in your immediate future...provided you are not a vegetarian. In that case, I suppose a deadfall trap would also work for a tomato, provided it happened to be rolling downhill and it were a rather large tomato. However, no self-respecting man ever hunted for a tomato, and neither should you.

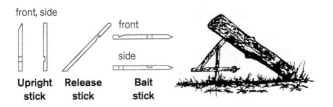

front, side

Upright stick

Release stick

front

side

Bait stick

Note: Most likely, your scent will deter animals from the trap for some time. Take care to not sweat on or near the trap. It may be best to pre-cut and test the assembly of the trap away from the area where it will be used. Also, approach the trap area upwind of the animal path, if possible.

CUTTING THE FIGURE-4

The figure-4 deadfall is so called because of the trigger mechanism, which is set in the shape of the numeral 4. To assemble the trigger, you'll need three sticks, each with a ½-inch diameter or larger, depending on the weight of the deadfall, with one of the sticks being longer than the others (this will be your bait stick). And, of course, you'll need a trusty pocket knife.

Lay the sticks out so that they make a figure four, with the longer stick forming the horizontal portion. Notches will be cut in the sticks to allow them to fit together, but laying them out in advance will give you an idea of where you need to cut the notches.

The support stick. The first stick will be upright and will support the weight of your deadfall object, generally a flat rock or hefty piece of wood. Cut a notch at the end of this stick and set it aside.

The hinge stick. This stick will be angled and touch both the support stick and the bait stick. At one end, cut a notch similar to the one in the support stick. On the other end, at the start of the last third of the stick, cut another notch. The notched end of the support stick will fit into this notch. It should not be a tight fit; just something so the sticks can make contact without slipping.

The bait stick. This stick will be horizontal and will make contact with both the hinge and support sticks. Near the end of the stick, cut a notch just as you did on the hinge stick. Where the support stick will meet the bait stick, you'll need to cut a square notch in both sticks so that the two can fit together. Once again, this should be a loose fit, but it is important to make the notches square, especially on the support stick, otherwise the trigger may not be steady enough to set.

The deadfall weight. The weight of your deadfall object needs to be approximately three times that of your prey. How much does a rabbit weigh? I don't know, but probably not as much as that big rock over there!

SETTING THE TRAP

Before setting the trap, test it out and make adjustments as needed so that the trigger trips with the slightest touch. Once you have it, bait the end of the appropriately named bait stick, set the support upright, and rest the hinge stick on the support notch. Lean the deadfall object on the hinge stick, but don't let it take the full weight just yet. While holding the deadfall, support, and hinge in place, place the bait stick in place and slowly allow the trigger to bear the weight of the deadfall.

Note: Don't press the support stick in the ground, as this will act as a column and brace the falling weight. There's a reason no one calls it a "dead lean-to."

MAKING A PRONGED FISHING SPEAR

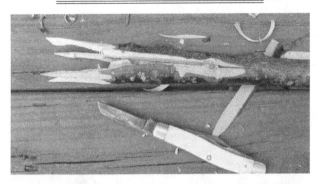

Catching a fish in the wild is no easy matter. Without a hook, line, and bait, getting a bite is going to be tough. Furthermore, if your survival depends on fish, then you'll need to have a fair share to sustain you. If there is a stream nearby or shallow water, you're in luck; fish can be lured and hemmed in fairly easily. However, they can be slippery little devils. This is where a fishing spear can be really helpful.

To make the fishing spear, you'll need a stick about 1 inch in diameter, some cordage (vines will work), a smaller stick, and your trusty pocket knife.

1. Split the stick in the center, vertically, so that you have a good separation of wood a few inches down. To do this, you can tap the knife blade into the stick with another stick. Sticks are great like that.

Perform the same task again, but this time cut perpendicular to the previous cut, so that the end of your stick is split into four pieces. These will form the prongs of your spear.

2. Shove another small piece of wood down the center of your four-pronged stick. This will separate the prongs, causing them to flare out.

3. Using your cordage, wrap up the pronged end so that only a few inches of the prongs are sticking out. This will keep your prongs from splaying out further and will also keep your inner stick from popping out.

4. Sharpen each of the four prongs to a long, fine point, making sure to notch a hook in the points as well. This will prevent the fish from slipping off the end of the spear.

5. Hunt and eat!

You may wish to remove one of the prongs so that you only have three, and depending on the size of the fish, you may want to adjust the size of the spear. The goal is to catch the fish, not destroy the meal.

HOW TO SKIN A RABBIT

Once you've caught and killed your wild game, you're going to need to process it for cooking. Skinning small game is very easy. The hardest part is getting over the idea of what you are doing, though if you are hungry enough, that won't be a problem.

To skin any animal, a sharp knife is paramount. There are a few things that will not only cause frustration, but will also taint the meat: a dull knife, animal hair, and urine or feces. A dull knife is a problem because it makes everything else harder, which usually ends up in mistakes, such as cutting things you don't intend to. If you are in a long-term survival scenario, keeping your blade sharp is going to be of key importance. If you don't have a sharpener, a smooth stone and water will get you by. But, it's best to start with a sharp blade and only use it when absolutely necessary.

1. Kill a rabbit. Easy, right?

2. Hang the rabbit by its hind legs. You can do this with a bit of cordage and a tree limb (or wrap

the cordage around the tree, if you have plenty to spare.) A slipknot is ideal here. Having the rabbit hanging allows both hands to be free.

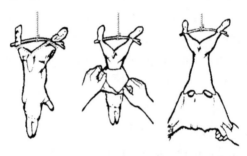

3. If you have a spey blade, use it here. Slice around the ankles of the hind legs so that you're through the fur and the skin.

4. If you have a clip point, use it here. With the point of the blade, puncture a hole in the inner thigh and slice up toward the ankles, where you made your previous cut. This frees up the leg and allows you to get a hold on the coat. Do the same to the other side so that both thighs are exposed, and begin pulling and cutting the coat away.

5. Continue cutting, using any blade you like, taking care not to contaminate the meat with hair or puncture the abdomen. Once you get down to the rib cage, you should be able to pull the coat free toward the neck.

6. You can either continue working the arms free, or take the rabbit down and cut the feet and the head off.

Once the coat is off, you can see how things are put together and how to take them apart. Field dressing the rabbit (taking out the insides) can be done at this point, assuming you want to use the entire rabbit. If possible, use a clip point to make a puncture in the abdomen just below the sternum (where the ribs meet). Once you have a hole large enough to fit two fingers in, use your fingers to press down the insides while you continue cutting down the abdomen wall toward the pelvis. If urine gets on the meat, it's not poisonous, just nasty and can taint the taste if it stays on too long. If this happens, simply give the rabbit a bath (this is recommended anyway).

Once the rabbit is opened up, take everything out, cutting free the esophagus and the colon (not pretty, but necessary).

If you are up on your anatomy, the heart and liver of a rabbit can and should be cooked and eaten. In fact, in a survival scenario, as much of the rabbit should be eaten as possible, even the bones. Rabbits don't have very much meat, so bone marrow, liver, and other organs are key to getting the nutrients you'll need to stay alive.

THE PROPER WAY TO START A FIRE

Once you have your game, you're halfway there. A fire is not only needed to cook your meat and purify drinking water, but it is a serious boon to the spirit. For this scenario, you'll need to use the striker method, meaning you'll need a magnesium fire starter, which should be packed into any out-of-doors backpack.

Step 1: Build a "bird's nest" of dry tinder: bark, twigs, leaves, etc. Gather small sticks and increasingly larger sticks to have at the ready. You can build a teepee structure with the twigs, if you like. The bird's nest would fit inside the teepee so that when it's lit, the larger pieces are ready to go. This can also be handy if you have high winds; the teepee structure can be positioned so that it blocks some of the strong winds.

Step 2: If using a magnesium stick, take the flat edge of your pocket knife and scrape off a pile of shavings onto a dry leaf. This can be done inside the bird's nest under the teepee, or it can be done outside, which is easier, and moved into the nest later. Use the edge of the blade closest to the handle and scrape. It's best if you can hold the magnesium stick against a rock while doing this. Otherwise, it tends to bounce, and the precious shavings go everywhere.

Step 3: If necessary, move the leaf to the nest, with the shavings piled up as much as possible. Here comes the trick. You're going to use your pocket knife to scrape against the flint rod, which is usually attached to the magnesium stick. Instead of pushing the blade down toward the pile of magnesium, hold the blade stationary and bring the flint rod toward you! This will prevent the blade from knocking against the leaf and sending your incendiary shavings flying. It will, however, still send a shower of sparks toward the magnesium.

Pro tip: Test the flint striking several times, away from the real thing, before trying it in the wild. Starting a fire is frustrating when you're tired, hungry, and possibly injured. Take your time, and be methodical.

MAKING A FUZZ STICK
FOR FIRE STARTING

Fuzz sticks, also known as feather sticks, are a tried-and-true means of getting a fire going. These are especially handy when the ground, and all of your bird's nest materials, are damp. If trying to light a fire with sticks larger than the diameter of your pinky, fuzz sticks can be a lifesaver.

For this survival tip to work, you'll need a trusty pocket knife, of course, and a few larger sticks that are nice and dry—dead wood that is still attached to a tree is great for this.

The goal here is to partially shave off the wood from a stick so that the shavings remain attached and curl up on top of each other. The end result should look something like a Christmas tree.

Firmly holding the stick in your non-dominant hand, with one end of the stick pressed against a solid surface, take your pocket knife and shave the wood as if you are trying to take off just the bark of the limb. Stop just before the shaving comes loose. Do this again in the spot you just shaved, this time curling up the bare, and hopefully dry, wood. The second shaving should curl up against the first. The thinner the shavings, the better.

Repeat this process, working your way around the stick until you have many curled shavings bundled up on the stick.

Fuzz sticks aid in lighting a fire because they create lots of pieces of dry wood in close proximity, with plenty of airflow in between them. To light your fuzz sticks, follow the process of lighting magnesium, but instead of placing your leaf with magnesium pilings on a bird's nest, simply make a teepee from your collection of fuzz sticks and place the leaf underneath.

SELECTING THE RIGHT POCKET KNIFE FOR TACTICAL ENCOUNTERS

Unlike a pistol, for which one can obtain a concealed carry permit, a knife has no such permit. Nor is there legal training on how to use them, or on when force is justified. In other words, using knives for self-defense is not regulated except on a case-by-case basis, in a court of law. Still, there are unique considerations for choosing a tactical knife that differ from selecting a pocket knife for survival.

When selecting a survival or tactical pocket knife, quality is still key. The knife must perform when it is needed most. However, a tactical pocket knife is typically going to be used in a burst of self-defense, rather than in a long-term survival situation. In this case, speed of deployment (opening the blade), as well as puncture ability, grip, and raw cutting power, are all going to be paramount. Additionally, blade shape and length are more important for a tactical knife than for an all-around survival knife.

Just as with survival, the scenario in which a knife would be used tactically will likely be thrust upon you in an instant. Having a knife that meets most of the likely scenarios will be key to staying alive or keeping someone else alive.

WHEN HUMANS
(OR ZOMBIES) ATTACK

Most likely, the first scenario that comes to mind is that of a human threat. Movies, no doubt, have a lot to do with our perception of knife use in hand-to-hand combat; maybe you picture an assassin quickly slitting the throat, then quietly hiding the body in nearby bushes. Real life doesn't unfold like that, and an engagement of knives should be avoided at all cost. Pulling a knife on someone, even as a gesture to show you are willing to defend yourself, can be considered a deadly threat, and the person that you were trying to scare away may be justified in using any force necessary to defend themselves, which could include killing you. So, yeah, it's not a good idea to use a knife for

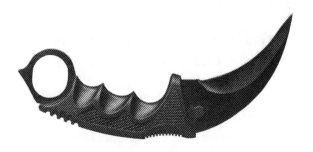

that purpose. A knife, as with a firearm, should only be drawn if you are willing to use it.

In the unlikely event that you need your knife for self-defense against a person, you will want something that can deliver the greatest amount of damage, which means cutting quickly through layers of clothing and skin, and severing arteries. For this specific purpose, a karambit style blade is ideal. Like an eagle's talon, the karambit has a long hook shape. Its sharp point combined with a curved edge work like a hawk's bill blade, but rather than being the go-to for a gardener, the karambit is designed to quickly puncture and tear at flesh. A drawback, however, is that the practical uses for this blade are fairly limited in everyday life, making it a style of blade most would not carry. Still, having one in reserve is not a bad idea.

WHEN DOGS (OR ZOMBIE DOGS) ATTACK

If you were to walk around the modern suburban neighborhood, you would likely see people walking with canes, though these canes are not being used as an aid. Rather, people carry canes and sticks in the event that an off-leash dog will attack. Unfortunately, these scenarios are all too common. Untrained, mistreated, and neglected dogs are more likely to escape their owner's confines and end up harassing those trying to catch a bit of sunshine.

You don't want to be in a situation where you are defending yourself against an attacking canine with a pocket knife. The challenges there are many. Assuming yelling, kicking, kneeing, and hitting the dog do not work, you will still need to reach for your knife, most likely while being bitten.

Dogs attack in a few different manners. Some run in and slash and then dash away; these are the worst. Others go for the jugular. They will do this by either going for your face in a leap (which is usually how your forearm gets involved), or they will go for your legs, and then once they have you on the ground, they'll go for your throat. The natural reaction is to pull away or run away, but if you are going to use a knife to save your life, you have to keep Spot (or T-Bone) uncomfortably close.

Assuming your forearm is lodged in the dog's mouth, you will want to press hard toward his jaws—as if you are trying to press your forearm further in, rather than trying to pull away. This prevents tearing, and also decreases the dog's ability to clamp down. It also gives you the advantage in terms of size and control of the situation. If possible, get the dog on the ground with your knees on the animal. You will have to move quickly to put a knife into the animal. I'm not going to tell you how to kill a dog—that's not the purpose of this book—but I would suggest multiple stabs. In this case, a tanto blade, rather than a karambit, would be ideal.

Once again, no one should ever want to be in this scenario and it should be avoided at all cost. In 99% of cases, standing your ground, yelling, stomping, and kicking will get the job done. Most likely, a knife would only come into play when a child is being attacked and you aren't able to get the dog off through other means. God have mercy on the dog that attacks a mother or father's child, for they will have none.

HAIRY SITUATIONS

The most likely scenario for using a tactical knife is going to be getting out of a bad spot. For example, you might have just a moment to cut a rope before someone's arm gets taken off, or to cut a seatbelt, etc. In these cases, an all-around pocket knife will likely work, but a quickly deployed, razor-sharp pocket knife can make all the difference. While there are not many scenarios where a deep puncture is needed, the tanto blade is still a fine style to carry. Tantos have a straighter edge that makes them better for quick, long cuts than, say, drop points, which tend to slide rather than cut.

How Is the Grip?

Tactical situations are going to be high intensity, and the likelihood of sweat on your hands is high. I've seen a number of tactical knives that save weight by using a skeletal handle. While they may look neat, the smooth surface and lack of contact with the hand means poor grip. Be sure that your tactical pocket knife has a grip that will give you a solid hold even, and especially, when your hands are wet. All-metal handles are not your friend. A composite handle with some surface texture will go a long ways toward making sure you don't lose your knife when you need it most.

POCKET KNIFE THROWING TECHNIQUES

What man doesn't imagine himself in something of the following scenario: You're standing in line at the bank or coffee shop and in walks a suspicious-looking character. You feels the hairs prickle on the back of your neck and you instinctively reach for your pocket knife—you know, the one you've carried since "the war." Just as the punk draws his gun, you flick open your blade and with a snap of the wrist, you throw the knife into the bad guy's hand (or maybe throat or eye, depending on the vulgarity of your imagination and the number of Tarantino films you've watched). Just when people realize the threat has been neutralized and begin looking around for their savior, you and your knife are nowhere to be found.

In reality, that kind of stunt would likely land you in jail, but it is one for the imagination. Our imagination fuels our questions of "What if?" and "Is that even possible?" and leads us down the road of becoming more prepared than we really need to be. Of course, this is part of the fun in being a guy, and part of the fun of owning a knife. To be honest, pocket knives are not ideal for throwing, but the chances of carrying a proper throwing knife on your person is not likely. So in this case, the ability to throw a pocket knife is still of greater value than that of knowing how to throw a knife you do not have.

SELECTING A POCKET KNIFE FOR THROWING

Unlike the selection of a pocket knife for survival or tactical purposes, there are characteristics one must take into consideration that are unique to a throwing knife.

- The blade must lock

- The blade and handle should be evenly balanced

- The blade shape should be conducive to puncturing hard surfaces (tanto, spear, or drop point)

- The frame and mechanisms should be solid and ideal for impact (screws are a no-no)

- The knife should be fairly inexpensive

The last point, about the knife being inexpensive, is rather key. Learning to throw a pocket knife will undoubtedly mean a good deal of wear and tear on the knife. The necessity of using the same style of knife to become proficient will mean purchasing the same knife a few times. It is possible to become well-adapted to throwing a cheaper knife, then settling on a higher-end knife of similar shape, style, and weight.

BUILDING A QUICK TARGET

There are numerous examples of building a quick throwing knife target online, but the basic concept is to start with a soft and inexpensive wood, such as pine two-by-fours. Lay eight boards down side by side to create a wall. Then, place two or three two-by-fours perpendicular to these to create a brace on the back. Secure the boards with screws from the back-bracing two-by-fours so that no screws are exposed on the front of the target. This creates the striking wall, and allows for overly worn two-by-fours to be removed as needed.

Once you feel comfortable with throwing, you may want to switch to an end-grain target. The end-grains (the ends of a board) are harder on a new knife-thrower and his knife, but are more resilient to knife strikes.

THE TRADITIONAL THROW

Any proficient knife thrower is to be admired, for the skill is a tough one to master. Not only does he need to be accurate, but he instinctively calculates the number of spins (or even half spins) necessary to strike the target with the point of the knife. This is no easy feat. It may take months to become merely competent at this skill, even with a professional throwing knife at measured distances from a stationary target. Adapting this to different knives in truly tactical scenarios will likely take years. However, this is not to say that it isn't a good deal of fun to try your hand at it, and you may find you have the knack sooner than you expect.

The traditional knife-throwing method, also called a spin throw, involves two different gripping techniques. One or both may be used as fits the scenario, but it is best to be consistent when learning. Gripping the handle or the blade fully is called the hammer grip. But, because most pocket knives do not have smooth handles (there are usually some indents for the fingers) and short blades, I recommend using the pinch grip. With the blade extended and locked, pinch the blade firmly between the forefinger and thumb. It is not necessary to pinch only the tip of the blade; in fact, you can pinch a larger portion of the blade if you find that more comfortable. Remember, consistency is key here.

1. Stand 6 or 7 feet from your target. Mark the spot so you don't have to guess at the distance. You can certainly stand closer and have good results, but you risk the knife bouncing back and stabbing you in the whatnots. So stand back, and practice like a pro.

2. Put the same foot as your throwing hand forward so that you are in a fighting stance. Point the elbow of your throwing hand at the target.

3. Imagine that your shoulder and elbow are locked in place and that your elbow will function merely as a hinge. Bring your forearm back so that the handle of the knife is even with the top of your ear.

4. Keeping your wrist straight and elbow pointed at the target, extend your forearm and release the knife when your arm locks.

Most likely you'll find that the knife doesn't stick on the first try…or the second or third. Once you are sure of your throwing consistency, take a half step back, and try again. Continue until you find a distance that allows you to stick the target every time. At this point you can focus on aim, and also change up your grip on the knife and see if moving a bit closer or farther away yields consistent results. Once you are comfortable with throwing and aiming, remove your distance marker and see if you can intuit the distance and proper grip and release. The goal with knife throwing is for it to become second nature, where you're instinctively throwing and hitting your target.

THE COMBAT THROW

A favorite throwing technique for close range is the combat, or no-spin, throw. This technique is popular with throwers of Japanese darts, known as kunai, as well as knife throwers of all types. As the name suggests, the goal is to throw the knife so that it flies straight, as does a dart, and does not spin. This technique works well for any knife that does not have a full guard and allows the forefinger or middle finger to rest along the spine of the blade. Luckily, this suits pocket knives well.

Performing a no-spin throw is all about the grip of the knife and the amount of pressure placed on the knife upon release. This will become more clear as you move through the steps.

1. Stand 3 feet or less from the target. The risk of bounce back still exists, but is less likely with this throwing technique.

2. Start with the blade locked and extended, of course, and hold the knife by the handle rather

than the blade. However, you will hold the knife so that the spine runs along the length of your middle finger. You may substitute this for your forefinger if you find it more suitable.

3. Put the opposite foot of your throwing arm forward so that you are in a fighting stance. Note this position is different from the one you take with a traditional throw.

4. Extend your arm, knife in hand, toward the target, and imagine the knife leaving your hand as if it were shot straight out rather than flung. This is the goal, though performing this can be tricky.

5. Similar to the traditional throw, point your elbow at the target and cock your forearm back, and quickly release.

6. Rather than letting go of the handle, allow the knife to slide from your hand, using your hand as a chute and the finger along the spine as a guide.

Here is what happens when you throw the knife, along with some of the mechanics behind what makes it fly straight. When the knife leaves your hand, your middle or forefinger (whichever happens to be running along the spine of the knife) will provide downward pressure, tempering the momentum of the knife's spin as it leaves your hand. While it is nearly impossible to completely stop the rotation of the knife, you can dampen the rotation enough so that the knife flies a bit straighter for a longer period of time. Longer throws using this technique require throwing the knife at an arc so that the point hits the target as the knife begins to rotate. Closer throws, which are ideal, can be very accurate and with a great deal of force, hence the nickname "combat throw."

The combat throwing technique is pretty powerful, as you can throw the knife with full force at short distances. This technique works well with any sharp and straight implement, such as a pen or pencil, as well, making for a valuable skill in your arsenal of manly know-how.

CONCLUSION

*"To be always ready, a man must be able to cut
a knot, for everything cannot be untied."*

—HENRI FRÉDÉRIC AMIEL

The pocket knife. The sheathed sentinel of the work-man. An ever-present diplomat to a man's ruggedness and sophistication. The representative of our refined savagery. This noble implement is deserving of high honors, yet it will likely remain the humble adornment of field hands, handymen, civilians, and SEALs alike. I believe it is this state of commonness, that when passed down from generation to generation, gives so much meaning to the pocket knife. All of the years of work and of wear are bound up in a blade. The stories it contains can never be fully told, but can be felt, and a lifetime of manful duties performed hone the spirit of its owner.

This book is intended as a small token of praise for the pocket knife. The reader, now imbued with its history, know-how, how-tos, and respect for this revered instrument, is equipped to carry his own pocket knife in a confident manner and to carry forward its traditions and knowledge to the next generation.

For fathers, may this book serve to fill in the gaps of knowledge and respect that may have been missed in their upbringing. For sons, may this serve to spark the tinder of rugged boyhood in an age of indifferent adolescence. For men of all ages and seasons, may you be inspired to carry a well-honed knife, and carry it well.

PHOTO CREDITS

Photos on pages 114–17, 119–22, 124, 126–30, 151–54 © Mike Yarbrough and photo on page 184 © Summer Yarbrough.

The remaining photos from shutterstock.com

page 10 © Andrew Buckin

page 15, 20 © blewis49

page 16 © Jiang Hongyan

pages 17, 67 © Paul Orr

page 18, Vince Reilly

pages 19, 65 © Derek Burke

page 27 © NA image

page 30 © Sean Pavone

page 34 © bigjom jom

page 35 © samodelkin8

page 41 © Jonathan Vasata

page 59 © LezinAV

page 62 © MyImages - Micha

page 63 © Albert Lozano

page 64 © SEKTOR

page 66 © Allison Achauer

page 68 © Corsair Marine

page 69 © Dragon Photos

page 70 © Photoexpert

page 71 © Photo Studio

page 79 © praphab louilarpprasert

page 88 © addimage

page 104 © Oleg Nesterov

page 132 © aragorik

page 143 © BW Folsom

page 144 © optimarc

page 145 © Sukpaiboonwat

pages 160 © 162, klyots

page 165 © suwatpatt

page 173 © Igor Zvencom

ABOUT THE AUTHOR

Having spent his formative years on the banks of the Hatchie River in the small town of Mercer, Tennessee, **Mike Yarbrough** yearns for the hardihood and old-school wisdom so common in generations past. He is the founder of Wolf & Iron (wolfandiron.com) and has a passion for helping men heed the high call of manful living. He now resides in Charlotte, North Carolina, with his lovely wife and two handsome sons.

Printed in the USA
CPSIA information can be obtained
at www.ICGtesting.com
LVHW020438091223
765516LV00003B/2